present into the future. His imaginative and critical synthesis is a fresh alternative to current philosophies of life, rehabilitating intuition as a philosophical method but tempering it with rigorous rational analysis.

The author

Michael A. Weinstein, a professor of political science at Purdue University, was the recipient of a Guggenheim Fellowship for 1974-75 and a Rockefeller Foundation Humanities Fellowship for 1976, under which this book was written. With special interests in twentieth-century thought, philosophical sociology, and Hispanic philosophy, he has written more than forty scholarly articles and the following books:

Identity, Power, and Change
Systematic Political Theory
Philosophy, Theory, and Method in Contemporary Political Thought
The Roles of Man (with Deena Weinstein)
The Clash of Perspectives (with Deena Weinstein)
The Political Experience
The Ideologies of Violence (with Kenneth Grundy)
Living Sociology (with Deena Weinstein)
Choosing Sociology (with Deena Weinstein)
The Polarity of Mexican Thought: Instrumentalism and Finalism
The Tragic Sense of Political Life.

The pen and ink drawing used on the dust jacket and frontispiece is by Don Carter, graphic designer with the Purdue University Press, who was intrigued by Weinstein's vision of the essence of human existence—expressing one another to ourselves.

The Purdue University Press
South Campus Courts—D
West Lafayette, Indiana 47907

Meaning and Appreciation

Meaning and Appreciation: Time and Modern Political Life

by Michael A. Weinstein

1978
The Purdue University Press
West Lafayette, Indiana

055315

JA
74
.W425
1978

Library of Congress Catalog Number 77-80424

International Standard Book Number 0-911198-48-2

Printed in the United States of America

To Marcia, my Ariadne

Contents

Acknowledgments

This book could not have been written were it not for the active, sympathetic, and intelligent collaboration of my colleague Dr. Deena Weinstein. Parts of the first chapter concerning the sociology of knowledge are drawn from our joint work, especially a paper called "The Sociology of Knowledge as Rhetorical Strategy." Although it is the custom to take personal responsibility for a work, Deena's contributions were so great that I am not sure where they begin and end in this case. Her critical spirit checked my proclivity to speculation at every turn and her interpretations illuminated the basic ideas that appear here. If there is imprecision and inconsistency remaining in my discussion, it is despite her vigilance and care.

I also thank the Rockefeller Foundation, whose Humanities Fellowship granted to me in 1976 allowed me the freedom and leisure to write this book. Ms. Diane Dubiel of the Purdue University Press deserves special thanks for her fine editing, perceptive criticism and insight, and concern for the work. Finally, I would like to thank the management of the Uptowner's Club in Chicago, Illinois, especially Ms. Debbie Dockendorff and Ms. Pam Trenckmann, for providing the congenial atmosphere and space in which most of this book was written. The club was an ideal place to write, because it offered privacy and amenities without the distractions of home or the depressing ambience of libraries.

Introduction

This book, although it is written primarily in the third person, is not so much an argument as an account of an intellectual journey that many thinkers have taken since the beginnings of the nineteenth century. The modern rationalist tradition culminated in Hegel's absolute idealism which made participation in a wider and more comprehensive meaning the highest aim of human existence. Almost immediately after its appearance, Hegel's system began to be attacked by people who felt that it did not express their deepest longings and who believed that it depreciated much of their most intense and significant experience. On a cognitive plane, doubts were raised about the presence of rationality and meaning in history; in the ethical sphere, the sufficiency of public morality was challenged by a vindication of personal responsibility; and in ontology, concrete human existence was defended against absorption of the self into a social process. Yet the attempts at liberation from rationalism were spiritually painful and almost always incomplete. Even those philosophers who dissented from idealism tended to initiate their reflections by inquiring into human existence in general and to place meaning as the goal of their lives.

Through successive generations of criticism, scepticism about the presence of a universal and substantive meaning for life and death deepened. At the turn of the twentieth century, the assertion of particular meanings was given up in favor of deriving meaning from the ever-frustrated search for

2

INTRODUCTION

meaning. A new type of wisdom arose that still rules the advanced thought of our time. This wisdom is based on the supposed priority of form over content, process over substance, relation over object, and method over result in human life. For example, the American idealist Josiah Royce argued that although one could not rationally determine the meaning to which one should be loyal, one could be sure that one should be loyal to loyalty. Royce's solution was echoed in different ways by most Western life philosophers who counseled the search for authentic existence, rebellion against the absurd, the affirmation of responsible freedom, the quest for a method in human studies, the defense of democratic procedures, inquiry into the meaning of meaning, and other variants of doubling up relations or forms. The wisdom of process has become the contemporary consolation of philosophy for those who have reflected critically upon the particular contents of their socialization.

The paradox of contemporary life philosophy is that the doctrines which claim to defend the concrete are the most abstract of all. Jean-Paul Sartre's existentialism, for example, dissolves the individual human being into a tension between the nothingness of *pour soi* and the viscosity of *en soi.* José Ortega y Gasset's vital rationalism results in vacillation between the poles of falling back upon oneself (*ensimismamiento*) and losing oneself externally (*alteración*). Jaspers's existence philosophy details the elusive quest for transcendence over the subject-object dualism. John Dewey's instrumentalism defends an open process of inquiry against the closure of any substantive axiology. Each formalistic doctrine reduces practical human existence to its minimum structure: the opposition of an active subject and an object in successive vanishing presents. In each present the subject must be reestablished to choose and act. The Spartan discipline of contemporary wisdom deprives the human being of any time perspectives beyond the present. Incomplete liberation from idealism has meant the struggle to create meanings for oneself and others in full knowledge that those meanings are contingent and transitory.

3

The journey to the dead end of the minimum structure of practice, in which the human being is alone and responsible, occurs during a century marked by the transformation of philosophical and religious traditions into ideologies and the emergence of totalitarian regimes and organizations. It is a journey that all serious thinkers should take, even if it isolates them from others and makes them appear to be ridiculous. One must encounter the problem of meaning in all of its depth if one wishes to understand the life that we are leading. Modern philosophy has raised meaning above all other goals and values. Meaning is bound to historical time; it is an achievement that justifies conduct. Philosophy can be satisfied only with rational meaning, that which can be demonstrated to be necessary and universal. The crisis in contemporary life philosophy stems from the inability to prove that any meaning is necessary and universal. Lacking rational proof, meanings can be accepted on faith, imposed by force or other social control mechanisms, or abandoned in favor of the formalist's search. In each of these cases the notion that life must or should be justified by an achievement is not questioned. Yet as long as this notion is held immune from criticism thinkers will continue to take the journey to the minimum structure of practice and find no exit from it.

A small number of thinkers in the post-Hegelian era have criticized not only comprehensive historical and religious systems of transpersonal meaning but the centrality of meaning in human existence itself. Miguel de Unamuno, Feodor Dostoevsky, Max Stirner, and Friedrich Nietzsche placed such experiences as the hunger for immortality, expiation, and acceptance of life prior to any rational meaning. However, only Henri Bergson undertook a full-fledged philosophical critique of meaning by associating it with spatialized cognition and contrasting it with the intuition of pure duration, which reveals a process of expression that is creative of meaning. Bergson's early work announced a philosophical revolution that would have made practice relative to the processes disclosed by intuition. His insight into the struggle between mutually complementary and antagon-

4

istic self processes had tragic implications, but Bergson was not a tragic thinker. In his later work he devised a vitalistic system of meaning that has been criticized and forgotten along with his valuable intuition.

The purpose of this book is to return to the sources of intuition so that a complete break can be made with the idealist tradition of meaning and a new life philosophy can be constructed to replace current formalism. The argument is not based on or a development of Bergson's thought. I make no attempt to follow Bergson's reflections or to constitute a Bergsonian tradition, only to recapture the intuition that informed his early work and to trace its implications for life and politics. Those implications have been derived from my own experience of the intuition and my reflections upon it, although my conclusions are often similar to those of such thinkers as Unamuno, Stirner, and Dostoevsky.

Although this work is primarily concerned with life philosophy rather than with the general conditions of knowledge, its intuitive basis raises epistemological issues that will not be addressed directly in the following discussion. The most critical epistemological problem that appears in a discussion of human ontology is how knowledge of the self by itself is possible. Phenomenologists, who among twentieth-century philosophers have given most attention to this issue, claim that consciousness is intentional: it is always consciousness of some object. Following this understanding, the self is not an object, but is only known through its relation to objects. The intuitive method that guides the following work departs from phenomenology, not in claiming that there is a standpoint of "pure consciousness" devoid of any content, but that there is an experience in which the self, which is ordinarily present as a synthesis with objects, is divided into two opposed processes. Each of these processes constitutes a "self" that comments on and judges the other one in accordance with standards inherent to it: each one, in a sense, "intends" the other. Hence, we know ourselves polemically through the struggle between the two sides of our being,

INTRODUCTION

which ordinarily are fused together and indistinguishable from one another.

The thesis that we know ourselves polemically has the advantage of avoiding the postulation of a transcendental ego, but it has its own difficulties. Firstly, it does not provide an explanation for how the synthesis of ordinary experience (what Bergson called the "practical viewpoint," anticipating Husserl's "life world") is possible. Secondly, it does not explain how attention shifts from one side of the self process to the other while maintaining its unity and continuity. These two difficulties are not resolved in this work; they remain for future inquiries into the foundations of the intuitively apprehended "immediate givens of consciousness." I would like to add that these foundations cannot be epistemological or ontological, but must be metaphysical, showing the dependence of our divided being and the philosophical questions to which it gives rise on the structure of reality. At this stage of the development of my thought I am prepared to comment on the structure of our being, but not on the structure of reality, if indeed it is possible to pursue a metaphysical project at all.

The primary implication of an intuitive life philosophy is that we are not essentially free, creative, or meaningful beings, but beings who *express one another to ourselves.* We must appreciate life and express it in images before we can create our own contributions or participate in meanings. The process of expression, which arises from the intuition of duration, is usually hidden from our normal practical viewpoint in everyday life. We are continually creating contexts for ourselves in the past-present-future, into which we insert our actions and possessions (including our more or less stable self concepts). The problem of life philosophy is to describe the processes constituting practice and to relate the values disclosed by these processes to active existence in the world.

The being who appreciates and expresses the contents of life does not exhaust the individual person of flesh and bone,

6

who is a *concrete durational being* synthesizing expression and projects-in-time, as well as autonomic drives and rational ideals. This unstable composite, the human being, has never been and cannot be the subject of political philosophy, which deals in the conventional or social self: the subject of rights and duties. The distance between the results of intuition and the demands of politics for restriction on the expressions that can be carried over into action is too great to be bridged by a theory of history or public morality. Modern thought has tended to locate meaning within the public situation. The individual person has been told to stake everything on a contribution to a historical community. The intuitive viewpoint shows that the deepest human concerns have no political response. This viewpoint discloses that political activity is only valuable if it encourages nonpolitical forms of solidarity such as functional interdependence and mutual appreciation.

The lesson that meaning is not the highest aim in life and that politics does not respond to our deepest yearnings is not an easy one to learn in an age dominated by Marxism, pragmatism, and secular humanism. It is, in one sense, an immoral lesson to teach when the drift of political life throughout the world is towards totalitarianism and terror, and when people need inspiration to resist power. The choice for a political philosopher is that between the Grand Inquisitor's miracle, mystery, and authority, and truthful report of the results of reflection. I have chosen the latter alternative, not without a certain sadness that I do not write in a time when I can confidently recommend a rational and collective hope. My intellectual life has been a journey through the systems of meaning developed by past and present thinkers. None of them has resisted either rational criticism or the demands of concrete life. Each of them, however, has contained a dimension of experience to appreciate.

Perhaps it would be worthwhile to ask for less from politics than moderns have tended to do. But such a course would seem to be suicidal in a politicized world. Opponents of an intuitive philosophy will point out that expression and appreciation are values realized by privileged individuals. As the Grand Inquisitor noted, people demand bread and meaning. Current theorists do not merely make the notation, but try to justify the demand. I am not certain that they are wrong. Yet I also notice that the people whom I encounter individually demand much more than bread or meaning. They wish to express themselves and assert themselves. They wish to love and be loved. And secularism has not deprived them of a hunger for immortality. A philosopher cannot do more with these conflicts and paradoxes than attempt to experience them intimately and determine as far as possible their relations to one another. This book is an effort to avoid simplification of human existence and to weave as many of its threads as possible into a fabric. Such an enterprise violates the political will to effective action and, if taken seriously, has the practical import of moderating politics. Yet it is not at all clear that the poor and dispossessed should moderate politics. The tragic sense of political life today is that resistance to terror and depersonalization seems to demand terror and depersonalization. Knowledge is not virtue. The deepest yearnings of human beings may have to be sacrificed so that others may have these yearnings at some future time. Miracle, mystery, and authority may be the means to truth at some later date. The moral continuity of means and ends is as much an uncritical dogma as their separation. The values that emerge from the evolution of modern Western thought find no easy or perhaps even possible political expression. Yet they do find expression continually in the relations between concrete durational beings.

I.

The Explosion of Meaning (1)

Among many other distinguishing characteristics, human beings are marked off from other creatures by the activity of creating time. The process of living in terms of time, or what will be called here "temporalizing," is perhaps the most noteworthy human achievement, although it is almost always taken for granted and is accomplished, for the most part, without conscious and deliberate effort. Not only do human beings create the homogeneous time that Kant held was one of the necessary forms of understanding, but they create multiple times that are heterogeneous with regard to one another and related in dialectical tension and conflict.

The time of everyday life, which may be distinguished from the idealized time of science, time based on the rhythms of biological life, the highly personalized time shadowed by death, and the modes of temporalizing that are accessible only through intuition, is not given *a priori*, but is an impressive construction based on painstaking collective endeavor and intertwined with the meanings that people give their lives. The time of everyday life, that which we most take for granted and that in which we plan our activities in and our contributions to a common life, is extremely fragile and can be dissolved into its warring components when the ends to which we are directed lose their attraction or are called into question either reflectively or practically. The modern era as a whole, but particularly the twentieth century, has been an age in which the time perspectives of everyday life have been gradually fragmenting and collapsing until the present

9

10

THE EXPLOSION OF MEANING (1)

when there is a profound disjunction between the official time frames of massive organizations and the personalized time perspectives of individual human beings.

The distinguishing feature of a human as opposed to a merely biological life is a meaning that integrates various pursuits and dynamisms. It has only been in the modern era that this principle has been widely acknowledged, because only in this age has the problem of meaning appeared with severity. Descartes, who initiated modern philosophy with his *Discourse on Method,* remarked about his "excessive desire to learn to distinguish the true from the false, in order to see clearly in my actions and to walk with confidence in this life."[1] Bewildered by the diversity of customs and unable to accept the uncritical and competing dogmas of scholastic philosophy, he "one day formed the resolution of also making myself an object of study and of employing all the strength of my mind in choosing the road I should follow."[2] Descartes's decision to fall back upon himself to find the road that he should follow separated modern philosophies from those that preceded them. Henceforth truth and falsehood would not be measured by a reality independent of the thinking being, but by the structure of conscious processes. Truth and falsehood about human life would be determined not by correct adaptation to reality, but by the efficacy of ideas in promoting the confidence that Descartes sought. Descartes's quest for confidence ended with William James's "will to believe" and Dostoevsky's Grand Inquisitor: "Without a stable conception of the object of life, man would not consent to go on living, and would rather destroy himself than remain on earth, though he had bread in abundance."[3]

The Grand Inquisitor's accusation against Christ, the charge that human beings are given freedom when they need meaning, is a major theme of the modern age. Coming at the beginning of modern times, Descartes experienced the fundamental predicament with which successive generations of thinkers have been confronted: the encounter with diversity. Descartes was impelled to philosophize by the

THE EXPLOSION OF MEANING (1)

collapse of the medieval worldview and the multiplicity of meanings revealed by its ruin. His "excessive desire" to distinguish truth from falsehood was not intellectual but practical: he wished "to walk with confidence in this life." He found that everything was in dispute in scholastic philosophy and that there was no rational principle for resolving the differences. He found that customs and beliefs varied from one nation to the next and "learned to believe nothing too certainly of which I had only been convinced by example and custom." Yet Descartes's appeal to his own reason did not provide him with a meaning for life and death and a way of walking with confidence. It provided him only with the certainty that he existed as a thinking being and, implicitly, with the freedom to travel or construct any road.

The Cartesian predicament may be defined as the absence of a stable and certain transpersonal meaning through which human beings can integrate themselves into a public situation. Modern thought about the human condition can be usefully interpreted as a series of efforts, all of which have failed, to reclaim the unified systems of transpersonal meaning that characterized previous eras. Towards the turn of the twentieth century, awareness of the failures grew more acute and a cultural crisis of meaning was revealed politically by the onset of totalitarianism and philosophically by such movements as vitalism, existentialism, relativism, and analytical philosophy. Dostoevsky's idea that human beings would not consent to go on living without a stable conception of the object of life and would rather destroy themselves than remain on earth has been collectively verified by world wars, genocide, and environmental poisoning.

The time of everyday life, when it is maintained, is a collective product that functions to integrate the projects and contributions of human beings into a context transcending the personalized time of the individual. The time of everyday life, which might best be called cultural time, is unified by a transpersonal meaning linking human beings to a past that happened before they became aware and to a future that will

12

occur after they die. The form in which cultural time is conceived is indifferent to its function of providing the vehicle for meaning. For example, cultural time can be conceived of as a cycle of death and rebirth, as a linear progression, as a dialectical spiral, as a series of ages marked by catastrophic events, or in many other ways without affecting its function. Within whatever spatialized form it is depicted, cultural time can be filled with meanings, or purposes, that show people how their activities and plans are related to a more extended unity. Without a secure system of cultural time, there can be no public situation, no community, no shared and fixed conception of the object of life. Along with the Cartesian predicament, in which all systems of transpersonal meaning are held up to doubt, has gone the collapse of cultural time.

When cultural time perspectives fragment and collapse, human beings are thrown back upon themselves as creatures who must consciously create time. Lacking a transpersonal reference for their projects, individuals tend to retreat towards a consciousness of time that is bounded by the limits of their physical presence or by an infinity of emptiness. In either case there is no longer a public situation to which human beings can make lasting contributions, but merely a confrontation of power in which human beings group together in order to impose contingent personal meanings upon others. The Cartesian predicament of being thrown back upon one's own resources in order to gain meaning is not merely the experience out of which the modern age was created, but the permanent foundation of the entire era to which all must retreat when attempts to recapture transpersonal meaning fail.

Just as Descartes stands at the beginning of the modern age and defines the basic predicament facing the individual in relation to the public situation, so Thomas Hobbes depicts the structure of interpersonal relations in that situation. Hobbes's description of the state of war is the political counterpart of the individual's encounter with diversity and struggle to gain transpersonal meaning. According to

THE EXPLOSION OF MEANING (1)

Hobbes, war should not be considered as a certain set of acts, but as a way of existing in time:

> For WAR consists not in battle only, or the act of fighting, but in a tract of time wherein the will to contend by battle is sufficiently known; and therefore the notion of *time* is to be considered in the nature of war as it is in the nature of weather. For as the nature of foul weather lies not in a shower or two of rain but in an inclination thereto of many days together, so the nature of war consists not in actual fighting but in the known disposition thereto during all the time there is no assurance to the contrary.[4]

Hobbes understood that cultural time is neither a series of instants nor a way of marking seasonal changes, but a perspective unified by meaning. He did not fully appreciate the public and communal dimension of all transpersonal meaning, believing that human beings basically needed the security to pursue personal meanings rather than confidence in their capacity to integrate themselves into a common life. For Hobbes, the public and communal dimension of meaning was a set of enforced rules by which peace could be maintained when individuals came into conflict with one another. He contrasted war with peace rather than with meaning. Hobbes's refusal or inability to provide more than a minimum, negative, and formal function for public activity is similar to Descartes's unwillingness or incapacity to do more than express certainty in himself as a thinking being. Both of these initiators of modern thought faced the modern situation of diversity and described it precisely, but did not offer a resolution to its problems.

A time of war, as Hobbes defined it, is one in which human beings are incapable of actualizing transpersonal meaning in the public situation because they are concerned primarily with establishing their ability to act within time perspectives transcending the present. The state of nature is not a counterfactual idealization, but an accurate description of the structure of modern politics, just as Cartesian provisional doubt is not a method, but a precise rendition of the level to which consciousness continually falls in modern times. Both

14

THE EXPLOSION OF MEANING (1)

Descartes and Hobbes believed that the desire for biological survival would counterbalance the destructive effects of the collapse of cultural time perspectives. With several centuries of experience with the modern predicament behind him, Dostoevsky rejected this hope and announced that human beings would destroy themselves without a stable conception of the object of life: "How to fit yourself and your work and its product into the institutions with which they connect most immediately, and through these institutions to fit your self and them into the total structure of the good life, is precisely the question of politics as it faces the individual"[5] (Elijah Jordan).

Descartes and Hobbes wrote in a period when the unified cultural time of the Medieval Age was collapsing and no substitutes for it had yet been devised. The quest for such substitutes and the active experimentation with those that have been devised has filled the time of war between the endeavors of the early rationalists to confront diversity and conflict, and contemporary efforts to cope with the strife between contending totalitarian organizations. The competing attempts to generate transpersonal meaning and new perspectives of cultural time have replaced the mere encounter with diversity of customs and beliefs with the problem of relativism, and the problem of composing conflicting interests into public order with the task of gaining freedom from organizations that themselves are the causes of disorder and combat.

Relativism

The problem of relativism, in its contemporary form, begins with Kant's notion of the relativity of knowledge to the structure of cognition. With regard to epistemology, relativity is the doctrine that knowledge is dependent upon the capacities of cognition that human beings bring with them to a knowing situation. This position is critical rather than skeptical. While it argues that human beings do not know the truth about

THE EXPLOSION OF MEANING (1)

reality, a single process of reasoning is acknowledged, to which all particular truth claims can be referred. Certainty can be attained about the structure of human reason itself, and there is confidence in science as a means of obtaining public knowledge about the phenomenal world.

Relativism constitutes a distinctive departure from relativity in that it questions the independence and universality of human reason as a means of attaining knowledge, thereby severing the last link of the modern era to its predecessors. According to relativists, the content and sometimes even the form of knowledge are relative to some factor beyond human consciousness; for example, one's status in a system of property ownership, some past experiences that one has repressed, the structure of the language one uses, one's nation or race. Relativists have been criticized on the grounds that they presuppose an absolute standard to support their judgment that knowledge is relative, or that their theory itself is relative and therefore has no grounds. This argument, while it does reveal a major philosophical problem in relativism, does not replace it with anything, and even more importantly does not disclose the reasons why people continue to find relativism more plausible than other available positions, despite its problems. The thrust of the critique seems to be that relativists should return to some earlier position that implies confidence in the ability of reason to apprehend truth. However, relativists are aware of these earlier positions and find them wanting because of impressive evidence that thought is indeed relative to other aspects of experience.

The chief originator of modern relativism is Hegel, who made the development of consciousness dependent upon the moments of the dialectical evolution of the Absolute spirit. Hegel is a transitional figure between Kant and the positivists and Marxists who perfected the evolutionary paradigm as a vehicle of transpersonal meaning. According to Hegel, history was the field upon which the Absolute was expressed. Various forms of social life (family, civil society,

16

THE EXPLOSION OF MEANING (1)

and the state) were correlated with the increasing self-consciousness of the spirit. Hegel's signal contribution was to transfer reason from the thinking individual, where it had been lodged since the Cartesian experiment, to history. By so doing, he attempted to restore cultural time perspectives, removing them from religious contexts of salvation and placing them in the public situation. To think in a Hegelian manner is to conceive of transpersonal meaning as a process of fitting oneself and one's work into the structure of the good life. The alternative, for Hegel, to basing one's life on contributing to the public situation is "subjectivism" or "unhappy consciousness," in which the individual is torn apart by abstract antinomies such as matter and spirit, passion and reason, practice and theory.

The specifics of Hegel's vision of cultural time, such as the idea that previous moments of historical development are synthesized into more comprehensive and organized unities, have been less important than the general notion that transpersonal meaning is found through a relation between the individual and historical circumstances. Once this basic conception had been formulated there could be and were endless variations on the theme. Any number of temporal images could be used to unify the diversity of contending meanings that Descartes and his successors had confronted.

Relativism reached its maturity when it was united with scientific naturalism in the nineteenth-century political sociologies. Positivism and Marxism did not unify historical development around the moments of spiritual activity, but coordinated diversity according to principles immanent to human institutions. They provided stable transpersonal meaning by guaranteeing contributions to the common life in terms of future public situations. The guarantees were supposedly backed by the scientific standing of the theories. However, by the turn of the twentieth century, the intellectual landscape was strewn with competing systems of transpersonal meaning rooted in historical interpretations, none of

THE EXPLOSION OF MEANING (1)

which had succeeded in unifying the public situation by providing a secure cultural time perspective. It became clear to such thinkers as Mosca, Michels, and Sorel that the definition of the public situation cannot be known with certainty because visions of historical circumstance gain and lose credibility according to the power and commitment that are marshalled to support them.

Modern relativism became complicated by the presence of competing relativistic theories, each one of which vied with the others for loyalty and allegiance. The completeness of each theory was challenged by the critiques of the others, while the universality of each one was discredited by its limited support. A hallmark of twentieth-century thought has been to reinterpret the relativistic political sociologies as ideologies masking the pursuit for power. While the ideological function of modern relativistic theories is indisputable, intellectually they may be conceived of as images of the public situation that can serve as vehicles of transpersonal meaning.

To consider a theory, such as Marxism, positivism, or structural-functionalism, as an image of the public situation means to analyze it as a construct providing people with transpersonal meaning rather than as a scientific hypothesis. Theories of society for which claims to scientific status are made are supposed to explain and predict the dynamics of human activity within public situations. However, when such theories are considered by the individual as descriptions providing knowledge of social existence and the destiny of projects, they become images of the public situation that are evaluated in terms of their adequacy for orienting action and their fruitfulness for encouraging it. Every political sociology can be conceived of both as a scientific hypothesis and as an image of the public situation. Considered scientifically, each relativistic theory tends to be deterministic, providing at least limits to the range of human activity. Considered practically, each theory tends to be voluntaristic, providing a series of options or possibilities for relating oneself to the public

18

THE EXPLOSION OF MEANING (1)

situation. The presence of competing relativistic theories of cultural time, none of which commands universal acceptance and each of which may be backed by organized groups seeking power, encourages considering them as images of the public situation rather than as scientific hypotheses. In this process of revaluation, claims to scientific standing are reinterpreted as guarantees of certain meaning similar to the guarantees offered by older theological perspectives of cultural time.

Despite wide variations in their representations of cultural time and the types of social and cultural determination that they define, images of the public situation all have the same essential structure when they are interpreted as vehicles of transpersonal meaning relating individuals to a past and a future beyond their personal life times. Each image provides an account of the significant groups composing the social order and the relations that hold among them, a set of values which supposedly are or should be realized in social life, and an orientation for action. Ortega Y Gassett expresses the image this way: "I am I and my circumstances and if I do not save my circumstances I do not save myself."

Images of the public situation are descriptions of the relevant historical circumstances to which the individual should be oriented and prescriptions for transforming or maintaining those circumstances. They are ways of fitting oneself and one's work into the structure of the good life. The most significant aspect of an image of the public situation, then, is the identity that it gives the individual with relation to a collective historical actor. Hegel, the great initiator of modern relativism, marked off the public situation in terms of "peoples," each one of which had made a contribution to the evolution of the spirit. Through their contribution to the collective project of the people to which they belonged, human beings could "save" their circumstances and thereby save themselves. In the Hegelian image the relations between peoples were marked by conflict and struggle as one attempted to bring the spirit to a higher order of self-realization

THE EXPLOSION OF MEANING (1)

while the others opposed it and, therefore, tempered it. Individuals were integrated into the public situation by discharging their social duties within the station that they occupied.

Later historical relativists devised perspectives of cultural time that contrasted and clashed with Hegel's vision. Marx, for example, substituted economic classes for peoples, the value of justice for self-conscious order, and the project of revolutionary transformation for obedience. The reactions against Marx's system of transpersonal meaning departed only in content, but not in essential form, from his vision. Classes might be replaced with interest groups or masses and elites, conflict might be opposed by competition, cooperation, or manipulation, justice might be eclipsed by freedom of choice or honor, and revolution might be countered by reform or resistance; but all of the competitors of Marx were compelled to follow his lead by attempting to provide alternative collective identities and projects as mediators of transpersonal meaning. In the sense that the chief medium of transpersonal meaning and cultural time is today the image of the public situation, Jean-Paul Sartre is correct in saying that we live in the "age of Marx."

In order to perform its function as a vehicle of transpersonal meaning, an image of the public situation must unify cultural time by offering a vision of history that is necessary rather than contingent. Philosophical critiques of such notions as historical inevitability and a single human history miss the point that images of the public situation have become the modern equivalents of religious systems of transpersonal meaning. Whether the demand of many human beings to have something permanent of themselves saved is universal or merely an aspect of Western culture, this demand is not easily expunged by noting the terrible consequences of political fanaticism and the contradictions involved in deterministic appeals to individual volition. The fact that many images of the public situation claim scientific standing does not mean that their chief function is explana-

20

tion and prediction. Hegel's attempt to rationalize history has been paradigmatic for later efforts to create cultural time perspectives, even those that have embraced pluralism. The structural-functionalist notion of an evolutionary development proceeding from traditional undifferentiated societies to modern multi-group societies is as much a unified system of cultural time as the Marxist idea of historical materialism.

Insofar as contingency, ambiguity, choice, and novelty are built into history, all attempts to make images of the public situation vehicles of transpersonal meaning will be doomed to failure by their exclusivity. Any theory of history, except a panhistoricism that would make every human project necessary to the fulfillment of an undefinable universal end, must select some groups as relevant rather than others, some relations as more fundamental than the rest, some values as more worthy than their alternatives, and some modes of action as more feasible or desirable than other options. Yet the principle of selection and, therefore, the system of transpersonal meaning and the perspective on cultural time will be arbitrary and contingent unless it is made to be rational and necessary by a drastic social surgery accomplished through the application of organized terror.

Had there been only one example of modern relativism, there might have been no cause to question the notions of historical inevitability and a single human history. The presence of competing relativisms gives rise to a kind of second-order doubt that Descartes did not have to confront. Descartes encountered the collapse of the medieval perspective of cultural time, not the violent competition of organizationally backed aspirants to providing unity to the human condition. Descartes, at least, knew his circumstances, if not himself. Today it is possible to experience extreme doubt about the very circumstances that one confronts. Ortega's notion that "I am I and my circumstances" presumes that it is possible for me to know my circumstances. However, Ortega himself never satisfactorily made that determination in his own case and concluded that authentic existence was continually

THE EXPLOSION OF MEANING (1)

inquiring about one's circumstances and one's place within them. Rather than merely stating that "I am I and my circumstances," he might have more accurately said that "I am I and my circumstances, and the perspective that I choose to take on them." Yet if the perspective that one adopts is at least in part a matter of choice, it is no longer an adequate vehicle of stable transpersonal meaning.

The competing modern relativisms have attempted to establish their necessity and universality intellectually by means of interperspectival debate prosecuted with what has come to be known as "the sociology of knowledge." Considered as means of establishing and defending images of the public situation, the major sociologies of knowledge are most fruitfully conceived of as rhetorical strategies of persuasion rather than as scientific theories.

The structure of interperspectival debate is to discredit an opponent's view by reducing it to the terms of the theory that one represents. It is often assumed that the so-called "classical" sociology of knowledge, particularly its Marxian variant, functions by claiming that an opposing theory is held because of the distorting factors of "social position," material interests, or "nonlogical" factors in the personality. While this view makes it easy to demonstrate that any total sociology of knowledge is self-contradictory because it must be rooted in interests itself, it does the classical sociologists of knowledge an injustice. Each sociology of knowledge has had an epistemological ground, or theory of social truth, based upon the relativistic theory from which it has been derived, to which opposing theories are held relative. Mediating between the epistemological ground and the perspective being declared false is a process defining "false consciousness" and either an implicit or explicit motivating principle for this process. The conditions for setting the personal motivator to work are often defined socially, leading to the idea that interest distortion is the basis of modern interperspectival critique. Actually, the definition of relevant social conditions or circumstances causing "false" perspectives seems to be

THE EXPLOSION OF MEANING (1)

subordinate to the epistemological ground rather than the reverse. Sociologies of knowledge are the philosophical defense perimeters of images of the public situation which have been developed because of the multiplicity of transpersonal meaning systems or visions of historical circumstances and cultural time. They are essentially philosophical, not sociological, critiques.

Marxism, which provides the model for the sociology of knowledge, shows the basically philosophical character of interperspectival debate. Marx's and Engels's critique of philosophical idealism in the *Manifesto* proceeds in two steps. Firstly, the social, political, and economic ideas resulting from an idealist perspective are criticized by a materialist philosophy. Secondly, the specific ideas under attack are related to class interest. The synthesis between philosophical analysis and sociological attribution is provided by political conflict. An intensive examination of the attack leveled by Marx and Engels against the left-wing Hegelians illustrates the subtlety, flexibility, and essentially epistemological nature of their method.

Marx and Engels attack "German or 'True' Socialism" more passionately than any other competing socialist doctrine. They begin by noting that historically "true" socialism stemmed from the importation of French socialist ideas into Germany and the consequent attempt of the German "literati" to annex the new ideas "without deserting their own philosophic point of view." This "annexation" took place by a process of "translation" in which the concrete content of the French ideas was removed and only the inert forms remained: "For instance, beneath the French criticism of the economic functions of money, they wrote 'alienation of humanity,' and beneath the French criticism of the bourgeois state, they wrote, 'dethronement of the category of the general,' and so forth."[6] The translation of the particular into the general and the temporal into the eternal gave the "true" socialist consciousness of "having overcome 'French one-sidedness' and of representing, not true requirements, but the requirements of truth; not the interests of the proletariat, but the interests of human nature, of man in general, who belongs to no class, has no reality, who exists only in the misty realm of philosophical fantasy."[7]

The critique of "true" socialism up to the point that we have brought it is primarily epistemological. Accurate knowledge of society is based upon perception of particular historical situations involving class conflicts. False consciousness arises from a process of "translation" in which particular judgments are generalized and then the general ideas are made to precede, logically and ontologically, specific situations. Essentially, the critique of ideology is an attack on the Platonic spirit, in which the forms of perception are made prior to their contents. This critique runs parallel to the analysis of alienation, in which the proletarian's labor is taken away from him or her and becomes a commodity on the market. In the case of false consciousness, the ideas created to explain and transform particular situations become translated into essences that define the limits of human activity. The process of translation is particularly clear in the example of the left-wing Hegelians who actually initiated their theorizing by generalizing an existent literature, but it is also the mainspring of utopian socialism which is described as a "search after a new social science, after new social laws" that are meant to create the conditions for a new social order.

The remainder of the critique of "true" socialism is devoted to showing how this doctrine represents political and class interests. However, Marx and Engels do not argue that "true" socialism was directly *caused* by economic conditions, but only that it *functioned* as a weapon in political conflict for supporting the German petty bourgeoisie. The basic rhetorical strategy of the Marxist sociology of knowledge is to decode or retranslate the abstract, general, eternalist, and static theories of its opponents into the concrete, particular, historical, and dynamic terms of historical materialism. There is no attempt to explain why any particular

THE EXPLOSION OF MEANING (1)

human beings became "true" socialists or why the human mind is so prone to the process of "translating." The critique is not an attack on personalities, but a procedure for making opposing theories relative to historical materialism by *postulating* the process of "translation."

The essential structure of the sociologies of knowledge that were developed to combat Marxism is the same as that of historical materialism, although the epistemological grounds, processes defining "false consciousness," and relevant historical circumstances are different. For example, Max Scheler, who coined the term "sociology of knowledge" and saw it as a political tool for resolving ideological conflicts, based his interperspectival critique on "an eternal *hierarchy of values*," the rules of preference of which are *"fully as objective and clearly 'evident'* as mathematical truths."[8] According to Scheler, the modern period represents an inversion of the eternal table of values, in which such values as intelligence, courage, and honesty have been placed below cunning, comfort, and pleasure. The mechanism that mediates between value inversion and the objective axiology is *ressentiment*, or the repression of envy leading to an affirmation of one's weaknesses and a detraction from the strengths of others. Those who are most susceptible to *ressentiment* are failures who invert values in order to overcome their "oppressive feelings of inferiority." Bourgeois *ressentiment* expresses the failure of the new business class to attain to the aristocratic values of the nobility that it displaced, while proletarian *ressentiment* reflects failure in terms of bourgeois society.

The structure of Scheler's interperspectival critique is nearly the mirror image of Marx's. The objective hierarchy of values performs the same function as an ontological ground for Scheler as the structure of capitalism does for Marx and Engels, while the process of value inversion is analogous to that of translation. In both cases the interperspectival critique is based on a claim that the opponent has falsified reality. What reality means to Scheler is, of course, contradictory to what it means to Marx and Engels. For Scheler, reality is denied when human beings turn away from objective values and base their activity upon the shifting judgments of others, while for Marx and Engels, it is denied when human beings ignore their particular social situation and define it in terms of universal laws and abstract essences. In both cases, however, "false consciousness" is linked to a *postulated* process (translation or inversion) through which opposing theories are made relative to the epistemological ground.

The debate between the Marxian and Schelerian critiques of knowledge cannot be resolved by an empirical test because it is concerned with the definition of truth and knowledge, with assumptions that must precede any empirical inquiry, and with recommendations that can only be tested in political action, not in a laboratory. Yet the debate itself is stalemated by the appeal of both sides to supraempirical processes. It becomes possible for individuals to take the Marxian and Schelerian perspectives alternatively and obtain contrasting versions of their circumstances and projects as well as, perhaps most importantly, their methods of self-criticism. Both of these visions of cultural time, along with the others that compete with them, are empirically tables of social value from which practical implications (revolution in Marx's case and resignation to superiority in Scheler's) can be derived. However, when they are considered as axiologies offering possibilities for individual commitment, they are no longer adequate vehicles of transpersonal meaning because their necessity independent of conscious human effort cannot be demonstrated. The debate between perspectives is thereby transferred to the field of political conflict and power.

Formalism

The dominant response to the problem of relativism in the twentieth century has been formalism, which may be defined as the attempt to make the uncertainty about transpersonal

THE EXPLOSION OF MEANING (1)

meaning and the search for it substitute for any particular and substantive meaning. Formalism takes as many forms as relativism, but is consistently characterized by the abandonment of any hope in securing stable transpersonal meaning along with the retention of the problem of meaning as the central concern of human existence. While formalism may not be the life philosophy of the majority of human beings in the world today, it has been the preferred choice of intellectuals who have encountered the predicament of competing relativisms. Formalist concepts range from Royce's "loyalty to loyalty," James's "will to believe," and Camus's absurd revolt, to Ortega's, Mannheim's, and Sartre's notions of "authenticity" and Viktor Frankl's "logotherapy."

The differences between relativism and formalism can be illustrated by analyzing Karl Mannheim's variant of the sociology of knowledge. Mannheim's undertaking may be characterized as a "metasociology of knowledge" in the sense that it is meant to provide a way of relativizing existing sociologies of knowledge by showing that they are ideologies (e.g., Scheler) or utopias (e.g., Marx). In Mannheim's work, cultural time perspectives become of overriding importance because there is no longer any possibility of substantive transpersonal meaning, but only the possibility of being appropriate to the present situation (being neither "ideological" and behind the present nor "utopian" and in advance of it).

The starting point for Mannheim's reflections is the intellectual crisis created by competing sociologies of knowledge, each of which unmasks the hidden motivations of their opponents. The "stage in which this weapon of reciprocal unmasking and laying bare of the unconscious sources of intellectual existence has become the property not of one group among many but of all of them" has not only destroyed confidence in particular positions, but "confidence in human thought in general."[9] Mannheim intended his sociology of knowledge to perform the functions of rehabilitating confidence in human thought by providing a new interpretation of

THE EXPLOSION OF MEANING (1)

objectivity and thereby "aiding and curing" a divided society.[10] Yet his analysis is plagued by a persistent ambiguity
stemming from his judgment that social science uses the
"same concrete concepts and thought-models which were
created for activistic purposes in real life" and his "relationist" epistemology involving the principle that "all of the elements of meaning in a given situation have reference to one
another and derive their significance from this reciprocal
interrelationship in a given frame of thought."[11] If social
science is necessarily evaluative and political, then the
situation defined by relationism is similarly value-oriented
and partisan. If the situation defined by relationism corre-
sponds to objective reality, then the concepts of social
science are not those created for activistic purposes.

In most of his analysis, Mannheim appears to adopt a
position of value naturalism, the doctrine that values can be
grounded in scientific inquiry. He critiques ideology and
utopia not on the basis of an alternative political position, but
on the grounds that they do not accord with the requirements
of reality. In his discussion of "false consciousness," Mannheim states that the "danger of 'false consciousness' now-
adays is not that it cannot grasp an absolute unchanging
reality, but rather that it obstructs comprehension of a reality
which is the outcome of constant reorganization of the mental processes which make up our worlds."[12] Mannheim's
problem is that he has no way of "determining which of all
the ideas current are really valid in a given situation" apart
from the descriptions and criticisms offered by the ideologies
and utopias that he has critiqued, because he has no perspective of cultural time and is continually attempting to
adapt his thought to present and undefined circumstances.
Hence, in his discussion of contemporary European ideologies, he advocates a synthesis of all of them, including
aspects of fascism. Of course, each ideology cannot be
synthesized with all of the others in detail, because the
ideologies are contradictory with regard to their visions of
transpersonal meaning. By implication, then, social reality is

defined by those aspects of each image of the public situation that can be harmonized with the others, lending Mannheim's supposedly dynamic analysis a static and positivistic cast. This "reality" is not apprehended empirically or intuitively but conceptually, through a synthesis of perspectives. Yet the project of synthesis is not logically implied by the notion of a reality "which is the outcome of constant reorganization of the mental processes which make up our worlds." Rather, synthesis implies a commitment to such values as social peace, reform, and democratic planning.

In Mannheim's analysis of "false consciousness," his attachment to sociological realism slips into a defense of being "realistic" in its commonsense usage. Basically, Mannheim has two criteria for identifying false consciousness. Firstly, an image of the public situation is distorted if it is "in advance of" (utopian) or "behind" (ideological) the present situation. Such a judgment is presumably grounded in a comparison of the image with the synthesis arrived at by harmonizing the existing perspectives. Secondly, an image of society is distorted if it appeals to exclusive absolutes. Mannheim does not apply the first criterion, which is temporal, because he lacks his own perspective of cultural time, leaving him only with the second, which is formal and eternalistic.

Mannheim traces the tendency for people to adopt absolutes to a supposed "need for intellectual and moral certainty." Ideologists and utopians are those who find it necessary to "seek a way out of this uncertainty of multiple alternatives." Such people "may be led to embrace some immediate goal as if it were absolute, by which they hope to make their problems appear concrete and real."[13] Absolutization is an "escape" from freedom and responsibility, a denial of authentic existence. Mannheim's sociology of knowledge, then, fails in its aim of aiding and curing a society divided by multiple systems of transpersonal meaning because it merely throws individuals back upon the present, which is determined by the dominant existing powers. It is as

THE EXPLOSION OF MEANING (1)

partisan in favor of the liberal-democratic state as the ideologies and utopias are partisan in favor of their political forms. Mannheim counsels a continuous effort to determine one's circumstances in place of any project relative to secure circumstances. In place of transpersonal meaning, he offers the absurd quest for a synthesis: " . . . Reality exists in a present. The present of course implies a past and a future, and to these both we deny existence"[14] (George Herbert Mead). "This feeling of coming to the end or the beginning of things never comes to an end and is always beginning"[15] (Robert Duncan).

Mannheim's sociology of knowledge reveals the chief characteristics of the formalist response to relativism: the substitution of the present as the basic form of temporalization for cultural time, the replacement of transpersonal meaning by the search for a dynamic equilibrium or synthesis of perspectives, and the rejection of group identity in favor of authentic choosing and personal transcendence. These themes and others, such as the uniqueness of the individual and the nontransferability of projects, reappear in the works of many of the important twentieth-century thinkers, regardless of their divergent intellectual histories and often antithetical views on specific political issues and even on key philosophical commitments.

The philosophical structure of formalism can be shown by analyzing the shifts that occurred between the last evolutionist philosophies of the nineteenth century and the first revolts against modern relativism in the twentieth. An example of late evolutionism with an idealist cast is the thought of Josiah Royce in which the vision of cultural time and transpersonal meaning that characterized Hegel's philosophy of the spirit is attenuated to the point that human beings are effectively thrown back upon the present and bounded by a vacuous and infinite eternity.

Royce defines human existence as the quest for the true and complete meaning of one's life and work. The heart of his idealism is the claim that reality is a set of purposive acts

30

coordinated by a single perfect act, that act which is coextensive with the absolute mind. The basis for this claim is the observation that the human experience of a present always displays the quest for completion of an intended meaning, even when that meaning is not fully conscious. According to Royce, in their moral lives, human beings never experience perfection, and in their cognitions they never comprehend an integrated totality of objects. Human beings can be certain neither of the ultimate end for which they are working nor of the appropriate means to achieve that end, although the bulk of Royce's thought is devoted to attempting to prove that they can be sure that there is such an end and that their strivings are uniquely necessary to secure it. There is always something acknowledged beyond the present, and the ground for that acknowledgement is the absolute embodying moral and cognitive completion. Human beings are alternatively condemned and presented with the opportunity to strive for the completion of their internal meanings by seeking greater understanding of the actual character of these meanings and of the means to their realization.

The quest for meaning is carried on through social relations which, from the idealist viewpoint, are primarily vehicles for this search. The other person is the source of, supplement to, and clarification of the individual's purpose: "Our fellows furnish us the constantly needed supplement to our own fragmentary meanings. That is, they help us to find out what our own true meaning is. Hence, since Reality is through and through what completes our incompleteness, our fellows are indeed real."[16] The individual's belief in the other, then, is logically prior to his interpretation of nature. Since the other is the initial source of interpretations of the world, Royce concludes that philosophical ideas are relative to the individual's quest for meaning carried on in a social context. Thus, for Royce, each human being struggles for perfection and is aided in this struggle by others. In this quest, ideas about the world are developed which serve as the common basis for realizing projects. These ideas are relative to the state of civilization, serve a pragmatic function, and are subject to revision. Only the quest for meaning, its partial completion in society, and its final completion in the absolute are invariant.

Royce's description of human existence shows that even in late idealism the notion of cultural time has been dissolved, leaving no mediation between the individual's present and the eternal and unknowable absolute. Royce presents what is perhaps the most minimal possible system of transpersonal meaning. Human beings may be assured that their contributions are saved, that their acts have meaning beyond their personal lives, but they must remain uncertain about the content of that meaning. In practice, individuals are placed in no different position than Mannheim, who used strictly sociological language and concepts, put them. The first duty that human beings have is to know their circumstances so that, in Ortega's terms, they can "save" them. Yet such knowledge is impossible. The only guide to the completion of one's meaning can be found in social relations, but the perspectives that are gained there are necessarily provisional and relative to the state of civilization. More consistent than Mannheim on this point, because he retained belief in the absolute, Royce did not hold out the possibility of a "perspective of perspectives" or a "relationist" epistemology that might synthesize contrasting viewpoints.

The only difference between Royce's thought and Camus's absurdism is the presence in the former of the absolute. Both Royce and Camus declare that human beings demand a response to their will to "unity" or the completion of the meanings. For Camus, the relation between the demand for unity and the lack of response is the absurd. Royce, it would seem, avoids the absurd by postulating the absolute, but this absolute answers the will to complete meaning only in the most abstract way. Certainly, the belief that one's actions do contribute to the achievement of a final meaning lends life a sense of security that is lacking for the absurdist. However, neither Royce nor Camus can remove from the individual the necessity of deciding what to do in the present, even with regard to the choice of whether or not to commit suicide. Royce's individual is assured of contributing to the absolute mind regardless of what projects are undertaken. Yet this individual is still constituted such that the restless search for complete meaning is inevitable. The human being somehow is incapable of drawing comfort from mere knowledge that the absolute exists, but must strive to seek greater meaning and wider appreciation of diverse experience. Such a life of striving as Royce recommends is not very far from the life of absurd revolt. The distance between the absolute and the absurd is very short and can be travelled in a moment.

Royce sensed the collapse of cultural time perspectives in the modern era and was concerned about it. Anticipating later philosophies of crisis, Royce found contemporary civilization to be characterized by a profound and disquieting dualism splitting the way in which human beings conceived of, and acted toward, the material world and the way they related to one another: "The narrow clearness of our civilized consciousness tends to make us materialists when we view the world apart from man, and sensitive appreciators of life whenever we consider our fellows. And that is why, in our own age, theoretical Materialism has flourished side by side with the growth of a wide Humanity of sentiment."[17]

The most important consequence of this split for human existence is an increasing alienation of the human being from nature, an alienation that later became the basis of Camus's absurdism. While the animist believed that all nature was vaguely alive, the civilized person has developed too distinctive an individuality to interpret nature as anything but foreign to all human beings. People no longer conceive of nature as "a link which seems to bind our lives, in a relatively external way, together"—a dialectical relation—but endow nature with an absolute externality and indifference to human projects. Along with the distancing from nature goes an increasing moral sensitivity, because the civilized person's

THE EXPLOSION OF MEANING (1)

conduct involves "an organized system of responses to a human environment that he acknowledges as mental, conceives in terms of its values and purposes, and views as a more or less clearly connected whole—a social order, such as is one's own country, or humanity."[18]

The reasons for the split between the two cultures—the world of description and the world of appreciation, physical reality and social reality—are found in the very humanization of life made possible by technological and moral progress. As human beings make advances in the arts and sciences, their practical relations with the material world become increasingly utilitarian—nature becomes a "socially significant tool" and the power to mold natural phenomena to human purpose becomes a prominent motivation. This progress is defined by enrichment of opportunities for human initiative and growing complexity of interdependent social relations, increasing the sense that all people are live and sentient beings. However, progress is a double-edged sword, because it also leads human beings to experience only those aspects of nature which are "rigid, uniform, predictable, explicable, and in a measure, mechanical." What begins as a conception sustaining projects for material advancement is freed from its practical motives and becomes universal, inflicting itself as a dogma and causing people to ignore those experiences of nature which would offer them greater unity in their existence.

Royce hoped that the split between the world of description (external meanings or causes) and the world of appreciation (internal meanings or purposes) could be cured by the cultural adoption of an idealistic interpretation of being such as his own. This, of course, did not happen in the twentieth century and could not even in the terms of Royce's philosophy, which threw people back upon the present and offered them no perspective on cultural time, but provided in place of one the eternal and unknowable absolute. Royce, however, was prescient in identifying mechanism and instrumentalism as the conceptions that would become dominant

34

in organizing contemporary life. Rather than becoming "sensitive appreciators of life," human beings in the twentieth century have treated one another ever more as "socially significant tools." In organizing the public situation, cultural time has been increasingly replaced by the homogeneous "clock time" of massive organizations engaged in social engineering and experimentation. Meanwhile, formalism, the derivation of meaning through the personal quest for it, has remained through the twentieth century as the only life philosophy surpassing modern evolutionary relativism.

Royce stood at the end of the line of nineteenth-century evolutionism, conceiving its essential form by denuding it of accidental contents and anticipating the problems of twentieth-century thinkers. The transition between nineteenth-century evolutionism and twentieth-century formalism can be grasped by comparing the thought of an Argentinian philosopher, Alejandro Korn, with Royce's. Korn's philosophy is chosen as an example here because it duplicates the basic structure of Royce's, sometimes even in detail, while it rejects evolutionary concepts and metaphysical postulates, such as the absolute. Korn, who wrote a generation after Royce, is one of Latin America's great philosophers, standing in the same relation to Hispanic thought as does William James to North American philosophy. He is the paradigm case of what is here considered to be a twentieth-century thinker.

The decisive shift from nineteenth- to twentieth-century thought is that from philosophies of mediation to philosophies of immediacy. While nineteenth-century thought was evolutionary, deterministic, and collectivistic in character, twentieth-century thought has been relativistic, voluntaristic, and personal. Korn commented that despite metaphysical differences, idealism, materialism, and positivism all had concerns in common with evolution and epistemology, rather than with immediate experience and axiology. Both philosophies of mediation and philosophies of immediacy are defined by the distinctive uses which they make of conceptual

THE EXPLOSION OF MEANING (1)

structure. Philosophies of mediation employ conceptual structures as bridges between some basic human experience and a realm of being beyond present experience. For example, according to Royce, present experience is characterized by striving towards a goal, neither the means to which nor the content of which is fully known. However, in this limited and alienated present experience, human beings acknowledge a metaempirical realm in the forms of a systematically organized totality of fact and a perfect realization of intended meaning. Royce takes these acknowledgements as indicative of the existence of an absolute which eternally experiences a single perfect act. Thus, the conceptual structure of Royce's absolute idealism mediates between present human experience and a beyond: the absolute mind.

Philosophies of immediacy, of which formalism is the major example in the twentieth century, employ conceptual structures as bridges between finite human experiences. Korn's thought is exemplary of this pattern because he confines himself to reflection upon "the content of consciousness—the concrete content that successively occupies it, not consciousness itself, which is an inaccessible noumenon. This content lacks stability—it is a series of states, a process, a becoming, or an activity whose knowledge we will call experience."[19] Korn finds in concrete experience an irreducible dualism between a subject and object in opposition to one another. This opposition is synthesized in action, but cannot be reduced in any way to a final unity. Eliminating the "Cartesian concepts of thinking and extended substances," Korn remains with "only a polarized activity in which the I and its opposite are reciprocal functions." He argues, following the pattern of philosophies of immediacy, that his position is "limited to empirical evidence and avoids the ontological problem."

The significance of Korn's empirical dualism is in the way that it relates the poles of subject and object so that they become nearly equivalent to Royce's world of appreciation and world of description. In the essay, "Introducción al

36

Estudio de Kant," Korn argues that Kantian dualisms can be made empirical by reducing the split between subject and object to the experienced opposition between liberty and necessity. Necessity is objective in that it comprehends the succession of facts linked by the principle of physical causality into mathematical laws, and excludes personal will. Opposed to necessity is the subject, defined as action, "or better reaction in accord with values and finalities that it promulgates as the expression of its will."[20] As in Royce's thought, there is a split between internal and external meaning, but for Korn this gap is bridged solely in present action, only to be continually reopened. The lack of a mediation in Korn's thought between the present and a transpersonal meaning unified by a cultural time perspective gives his philosophy of life a more desperate cast than Royce's had.

Korn considers life to be a continuous struggle for liberty in a world subject in many of its phases to inexorable necessity. He notes that if everything obeys necessity, the subject disappears, and asserts that the living conflict of consciousness is not an interplay of pallid abstractions, but a clash of antagonistic forces. While Korn acknowledges a plurality of ideals in human existence—well-being, happiness, love, power, justice, sanctity, truth, and beauty—presupposing the attainment of each of these is the creative freedom of the person. Liberty is the presupposition of all other values because it is the process of valuation itself. Not to affirm liberty is to submit to necessity, which is to eliminate the subject and to annul consciousness and experience. Korn does not say that the annihilation of consciousness is impossible, for if he did there would be no sense to his notion that human existence is a continuous struggle to affirm liberty and the other values that it makes possible. He merely states that the first act of valuation is the valuation that there be a valuing process.

In Korn's thought any of the security left in Royce's philosophy of mediation vanishes. For Korn, philosophy is essentially axiology (value theory), not, as it was for Royce, an

THE EXPLOSION OF MEANING (1)

interpretation of being. Individuals can no longer have confidence that their contributions will be saved. Rather, they are continually threatened with being overwhelmed by necessity, or what Royce called physical reality. Human beings are not charged merely with searching for their destinies; they must now create them in action out of their fractured experience. Philosophy has retreated behind the quest for meaning itself to the presupposition of this quest: the process of valuing. The first value that must be affirmed against a threatening universe is that there be a process of valuing. This is the last outpost of formalism, to which many twentieth-century thinkers have travelled, including Camus with his notions of absurd revolt and a quantitative ethic of experience, and Sartre with his opposition, so similar to Korn's, between the *en soi* and the *pour soi.* It echoes the call of Dostoevsky's underground man for the "freedom to be free."

Korn's thought reveals the consequences of basing a philosophy upon present conscious experience, what George Herbert Mead called "the philosophy of the present." Holding fast to the present, the human being must continually recreate the conditions for action out of the warring fragments of consciousness. The individual is never established with an identity, but is constantly thrown back upon the project of gaining a sufficient foothold on existence for other projects to be possible. The result of the absence of any secure cultural time perspective beyond the present is a life of struggle to affirm one's subjectivity and freedom against necessity. The demand for completed meaning is undercut and one is left with the demand that one be able to make demands. Korn escaped many of these consequences of his empirical dualism by identifying creative freedom with Argentinian nationality and translating the perpetual struggle against necessity into a commitment to oppose economic, political, moral, and particularly intellectual coercion, all of which symbolized necessity in the social order. Later thinkers, such as Camus and Sartre, drew most of the conclusions and introduced such terms as "the absurd" and "Noth-

38

ingness" into formalist vocabularies. Creative freedom appeared to Korn to be an historical advance. He did not note that creation that cannot be poured into an intelligible public situation is no more than a transient experience.

Korn's moral justification for a philosophy of the present was the virtue of "intellectual probity." One of his commentators remarks that Korn "remains serene inside of the limits of experience; he does not permit himself to flee from consciousness; if he did, given his philosophical convictions, he would have fallen into the serious failing that he denounced with so much insistence: a lack of intellectual probity."[21] Intellectual probity is also the essential defense of Camus's ethic of limits and of Mannheim's advocacy of freedom and responsibility, and remains the last defense line of formalism. Formalists have laid bare the structure of a conscious life deprived of cultural time perspectives and, having adopted the method of confining themselves to the concrete content of experience, have rejected as an attack on the intellect any attempt to restore transpersonal meaning. The formalists are, then, the new Cartesians, thrown back upon themselves after the successive modern failures to win unity from diversity.

> To say that man accomplishes nothing but that to which his endeavors are directed would be a cruel condemnation of the great bulk of mankind, who never have leisure to labor for anything but the necessities of life for themselves and their families. (C.S. Peirce)[22]

> We are all putting our shoulders to the wheel for an end that none of us can catch more than a glimpse at—that which the generations are working out. (C.S. Peirce)[23]

> If we are asked to die for our country, we must at least be allowed to believe that our country's good is the most important thing in the world. (E.H. Carr)[24]

Formalism returns to the Cartesian situation with the difference that what is certain is no longer the thinking ego, but present experience constituted by subjective internal mean-

THE EXPLOSION OF MEANING (1)

ing, objective external meaning, and their synthesis in action. The static notion of a division between thinking and extended substances is replaced by the dynamic concept of "a polarized activity in which the I and its opposite are reciprocal functions." The virtue of intellectual probity, or what later came to be called "authenticity," is the analogue of Descartes's rule of believing "nothing too certainly of which I had only been convinced by example and custom." Descartes, however, lived in an age of political absolutism in which there was still widespread acceptance of traditional perspectives on cultural time and transpersonal meaning, and in which the mass of common people had not yet been politically mobilized. He could separate his reflections from their impact upon the public situation and feel easy about adopting his provisional code of morals, of which the first maxim was "to obey the laws and customs of my country, adhering constantly to the religion in which by God's grace I had been instructed since my childhood."[25] The new Cartesians think in an era in which perspectives on cultural time have collapsed and in which they know that their reflections have political consequences, if not complete social determination. They form fragments of the "people" and often feel called upon to justify their social function, particularly when they operate within academic or other complex organizations. Hence, they cannot adopt "provisional" moralities, but must defend their commitments within the public situation.

One of the crises that formalism indicates is a fissure between knowledge and virtue, or more accurately, between the virtue of intellectual probity and effective action within the public situation. Collective activity demands time perspectives that transcend the individual's present and into which the individual must insert particular projects. Perhaps it is possible for an intellectual, who is protected from the most overtly physical social punishments, to confine time perspectives to the present, but this possibility is not open to the majority of people who are daily called upon to make sacrifices by higher authorities and who wish these sacrifices to be justified. The only satisfactory justification for sacrifice of the creative freedom so highly valued by the formalists has been the insertion of one's life into a cultural time perspective, whether mythical, theological, or historical. Philosophies of mediation performed the social function of providing such time perspectives, giving the philosopher a significant role in the public situation. Philosophies of immediacy, on the contrary, tear down and ratify the collapse of cultural time perspectives and systems of transpersonal meaning, causing the philosopher to be alienated from the public situation.

Of course, the formalists are not the only ones who have had their time perspectives foreshortened to the present. They are joined in this condition by many of the inmates of total institutions and probably by a significant portion of the "masses" whom some of them have opposed with such vehemence, but whom they ironically represent better than any other social group. The doubt and intellectual fastidiousness of the formalists is mirrored grotesquely by the desperate consciousness of present danger experienced by those who have fallen under the complete control of formal organizations. These latter are no longer called upon to *make* sacrifices because they have been *made* sacrifices.

The distance between the results of the formalist life philosophy and the requirements of the public situation have led to such attempts as Sartre's to declare an end to personal adoption of formalist thought ways until all human beings are free and there is a single human history. Sartre's Marxism is either a rejection of intellectual probity (similar to Korn's Argentinian and Heidegger's German nationalisms) or merely a facade, or a "vital lie," behind which he retains his critical distance from any substantive transpersonal meaning system. The notion that the only way in which formalists can enter the public situation is through the propagation of vital lies and by concealing the truth about human existence that they have discovered is a common theme of late-nineteenth- and early-twentieth-century thought. Dostoevsky's Grand Inquisitor, who offers the masses miracle,

THE EXPLOSION OF MEANING (1)

mystery, and authority in place of freedom; Ibsen's Relling, who in "The Wild Duck" provides people with fruitless projects so that they will not fall into despair; and Unamuno's San Manuel, the priest who becomes a saint by concealing his doubts and despair through encouraging faith in his parishioners; all of them are examples of formalists who "save" themselves and their circumstances by dissembling.

The destinies of these fictional personae are mirrored in political thought by the Italian elitists, such as Mosca and Michels, who argued that a "political formula" (a system of transpersonal meaning) is necessary to coordinate collective action; such revolutionaries as Sorel who remarked on the function of myth in building resolve for action; and most recently by the structural functionalists, notably Talcott Parsons, who have stated that systems of ultimate meaning, particularly solutions to the problem of evil, are prerequisites for social order. In the field of psychoanalysis, Viktor Frankl recounts how during his concentration camp experience he attempted to provide people with any meaning that they would accept, even the most absurd, just so that they would not give up on existence. Such attempts to fabricate meaning, either for moral reasons or to achieve insertion into the public situation, are not necessarily to be condemned. Rather, they are an index of the depth of the crisis in twentieth-century life philosophy.

Formalism has, of course, been opposed by many other movements in twentieth-century philosophy. All of them, except the branches of analysis, logical realism, and logical positivism, which have been attempts to remove the problems of human existence from the scope of inquiry, have been efforts to infuse older philosophies of mediation with some of the insights of philosophies of immediacy. Traditional religious perspectives have been revived by neo-Thomists and Christian existentialists, classical positivism has been continued by the pragmatists, Marxism has regained respectability by new attention to the writings of the "early" or "young" Marx, and the legacy of idealism has been

42

carried on by process philosophers and some phenomenologists. The hallmark of each of these perspectives has been to rehabilitate the free and creative person with internal meanings within the boundaries of the particular cultural time perspective chosen to provide the definition of circumstances. Most of these movements achieved their prominence after World War I in a reaction against what one commentator called the "passive eclecticism" of the philosophies of immediacy.[26] None of them has succeeded in unifying the diversity created by the conflict of modern relativisms, although each of them has helped to temper the absolutism of the perspective to which it relates and to serve as a rallying point for internal opposition to hegemonic formal organizations legitimized by nineteenth-century doctrines. Meanwhile, in the absence of a unifying perspective of cultural time, the public situation has been organized by formal structures setting their own time perspectives of system maintenance and expansion, and using the old relativisms as techniques for securing, in Talcott Parsons's terminology, "pattern maintenance and tension management."

Abstract Society

An image of the public situation may be associated with formalism's description of the contemporary human predicament. While the nineteenth-century relativistic images defined groups set in relation to one another in a meaningful historical process, formalism identifies deliberately planned organizations which display no meaningful pattern in their interrelations but the abstract quest for the means of control, stabilization, and expansion, such as wealth, power, influence, and loyalty. Between organizations there is conflict over dominance and advantage, while within them there is competition for position, privileges, security, and control between subgroups and individuals. Each organization may have an official function that it is supposed to perform, which

THE EXPLOSION OF MEANING (1)

is specified in its charter, but from the formalist viewpoint this public end is subordinate to the struggle to accumulate or at least to defend space, time, and resources for their own sakes. The primary organizational form is what might be called the "conglomerate": an organization that is flexible enough to perform a variety of substantively contradictory tasks, because its principle of unification is strictly quantitative (the degree of control over the space, time, and resources of human beings and groups). The multinational corporation in the economic sphere, the superpower in politics, and the multiversity in cultural activity are all examples of conglomerate organizations that organize human existence for their abstract purposes through their monopolization of the available facilities for gaining subsistence and meaning, and through their plans accompanied by the programmed administration of rewards and punishments (behavioral engineering, terror, blacklisting, bribery, and threats, among others).

The organizational image of the public situation is an ideal type, in the sense that it describes the political consequences of the dissolution of cultural time perspectives. When there are no cultural time perspectives providing transpersonal meaning, there is also no public morality beyond acting for the advantage or defense of the organization upon which one has become dependent for the pursuit of personal meanings or for sheer survival. In practice, of course, social activity does not fully exemplify the patterns of an abstract public situation coordinated by conglomerates with no discernible substantive purpose. Firstly, except in the case of fascism, which is paradigmatic for the formalist image, since it represents the only novel development in twentieth-century political practice, the extrinsic values of control and obedience are not the official legitimations of organizational programs. Instead, older religious or relativistic perspectives on cultural time are used to justify collective plans, leaving the formalist with the task of having to demonstrate that these perspectives function as myths. Often such

44

a demonstration is impossible because the programs do, indeed, represent the pursuit of a substantive public value. Secondly, the collapse of cultural time perspectives for individuals is not a total and generalized phenomenon. Many human beings, if not the majority, continue to adhere to older systems of transpersonal meaning, which allows them to be shielded from the problem of relativism and to act for purposes beyond the span of their personal or interpersonal time. Thirdly, not all groups have yet been fully organized into the system of conglomerates, allowing the possibility for belief in renovating and transformational movements proceeding from such collectivities as the "public," the "people," and even the "proletariat." Insofar as human beings have not become radically dependent upon conglomerates for their subsistence and meaning in all of the phases of their lives (the limiting case of a perfect totalitarianism), there is possibility for the kind of hope in collective change that is denied by the formalist image.

Yet despite the distance between actual political experience and the formalist image of the public situation, this image does constitute the base point from which all of the other images can be evaluated and towards which they collapse in times of intense conflict. When contradictory demands are pressed upon the state by competing complexes of organized interest groups, when there is large-scale withdrawal of support for established organizations, and when there is military danger to state security, the public situation tends to take on the characteristics of abstract conglomerate society, of which fascism was only the first and least sophisticated example. More rigid plans and tighter controls are instituted by organizational directors, and human beings begin to vie with one another to establish themselves in the present in order to gain the prerequisites for meaning: some space and time of their own and sufficient resources to undertake even the most minimal projects. As each organization is transformed towards the limit of a total institution (mental hospital, concentration camp, prison)

THE EXPLOSION OF MEANING (1)

everyday life progressively takes on the very quality described by such formalists as Korn: a struggle to defend the very possibility of pursuing meaning against necessity. Only in the case of totalitarianism, the necessity is not represented by the "objective" pole of experience or the "world of description" or "physical reality," but by the official time perspectives enforced by the regnant conglomerates, which subsume the world of appreciation under the world of description. Viktor Frankl's notion of the search for meaning, any meaning whatsoever, under the conditions of concentration camp life is the contemporary analogue of the Hobbesian search for power after power.

The new Hobbesianism implied in the formalist image of the public situation is analogous to the new Cartesianism characteristic of the formalist description of human existence. Hobbes confronted a situation in which traditional perspectives on cultural time were collapsing, leaving individuals without a secure means of relating themselves to the public situation and revealing a struggle for dominance by the groups that had fragmented out of the older unity. His political correlate to the Cartesian thinking ego was the sovereign, which controlled sufficient means of coercion to enforce rules that would keep human beings from destroying themselves. Such self and mutual destruction he thought was inevitable when people could no longer trust one another. Mutual distrust, or what he called "diffidence to one another," was the cause of the state of war. In the state of war human beings are continually concerned with establishing themselves in a present from which they can mount other projects: they are involved in a search for "power after power," for the prerequisites to searching for meaning, rather than with even the search for meaning itself. Hobbes's endeavor can be interpreted as an effort to define the conditions under which merely personalized time perspectives are possible. Today this same concern has been revived in the writings of the formalists, who describe the struggle to establish the quest for meaning.

46

THE EXPLOSION OF MEANING (1)

The new Hobbesianism differs from the old in that Hobbes confronted a situation of political transition and fragmentation while his successors encounter a state of war *within* and *between* organizations mobilizing space, time, and resources under official time perspectives (e.g., "five year plans") regulated by abstract values of advantage and accumulation and legitimized by official histories inherited from modern relativistic theories such as positivism, Marxism, and idealism. Personalized time perspectives cannot today be guaranteed by a sovereign monopolizing the means of coercion because it is the superpowers and other conglomerate organizations themselves that constitute a public situation in which many human beings are continually in danger of being thrown back into the present. The time of contemporary war is official time, defined in plans and imposed by a wide array of social control mechanisms including the mobilization of guilt and the fabrication of self-images along with more physical rewards and punishments. Hence, the problem of order, which so preoccupied modern thought even into the twentieth century has given way to its opposite: the problem of freedom. The problem of freedom emerges in periods of organizational crisis when legitimating systems of transpersonal meaning and the practice associated with them are abandoned in the bare search for control. Such situations have been recurrent in the twentieth century.

That there is a new time perspective which has replaced the older systems of cultural time in coordinating human existence has been noted by some contemporary thinkers, particularly traditionalists whose systems of transpersonal meaning are alien to the modern context. For example, Friedrich Georg Juenger has distinguished between "dead" or "clock" time and "life" time. He defines clock time as "lifeless time, *tempus mortuum,* in which second follows second in monotonous repetition," and notes that the precise time-measuring devices of the current era are not "ends in themselves," but serve "to organize time, to rationalize time, to measure out more and more sharply the consumption of

THE EXPLOSION OF MEANING (1)

time."[27] Clock time is the basis of the official time perspectives of contemporary conglomerate organizations which coordinate their plans in terms of measurable durations and seek to fit human beings and groups to their schedules. The importance of what is called "timing" in the public discourse of today illustrates the dominance of clock time as the key perspective for unifying diversity. "Timing" refers to the proper moment at which to introduce a programmed intervention into the public situation so that it will secure its maximum effect. This concept presupposes that there is some schedule that society is following which is delimited in terms of official events, such as quadrennial elections, party congresses, or board meetings. Even wars must be planned and fought with regard to official time perspectives so that opposition will be minimized. The tendency of conglomerate organizations is to attempt to monopolize the time of individuals and groups, to fill it with their programs, both in order to secure the extrinsic values of wealth, power, influence, and loyalty, and to eliminate any possible competition. Hence, Juenger remarks that the dominance of clock time "has brought about a situation where man no longer has time, where he is destitute of time, where he is hungry for time."[28]

A Mexican philosopher, Agustín Basave, has captured the hunger for time identified by Juenger under the concept of living "in time and for time" (*el hombre en el tiempo y para el tiempo*). Basave remarks that for "the representative man of today, *time* is not only a condition of life, but also a criterion of value."[29] The person who lives in time and for time is pledged to repudiate and combat the past and to accept only the present: "Placed in becoming, in the constant flux of being and nonbeing, temporal man attaches himself to a present that appears to monopolize life, installing the dogma of the superiority of the 'now' over the 'before.'"[30] Basave claims that individuals living in the transitory present attribute to means the value of ends, making the perfection of methods and techniques more important than the achievement of results and prizing the effort to attain to truth more highly than

48

truth itself. From Basave's Catholic perspective, the mode of living in time and for time is the result of the rejection of living in time and for eternity. However, his description of the hunger for time is consistent with the crisis of being thrown back upon the present revealed by contemporary formalism and the concurrent erosion of cultural time perspectives by conglomerate organizations.

In the conservative critique, clock time is opposed by life time. This concept is not defined by Juenger, who confines himself to stating that one who has leisure is not conscious of time, disposes of boundless time, and lives in the fullness of time. He adds that it is doubtful that in nature there are any uniform repetitions at all. Basave, who also distinguishes lived time from clock time, remarks that the time that one has to sit in the waiting room of a hospital awaiting the birth of a child or in the anteroom of a government office awaiting an interview with an official are personal and irreducible to any other times that different people live in similar circumstances. He also notes that judgment of the length of duration is often a function of the number of events with which it is filled.

The notion of lived time is used by the conservative critics as a weapon for attacking technocracy, which they believe inhibits expression of the most significant aspects of human existence, such as contemplation, enjoyment of nature, and the free pursuits of leisure. Perhaps most importantly they hold that the rule of clock time snuffs out individuality by failing to take account of the particular pasts of human beings when they are processed through organizations. However, the concept of lived time itself seems to be compound rather than simple, confusing a multiplicity of modes of temporalizing. Included in the concept of lived time seem to be such dimensions as the subjective judgment of the span of duration, the personalized time of a life shadowed by death, the time of biological rhythms and the life cycle, the perception of the quality of time (continuous, sporadic, cataclysmic), the "timing" of projects in terms of schedules, the

THE EXPLOSION OF MEANING (1)

forgetfulness of the passage of time, and the wide variety of modes of being-in-time, such as expectancy, hope, anxiety, boredom, transiency, and desperation. Lived time also seems to include what Bergson called durational being: the unique character of any experience merely by virtue of having been summated to the entire experience of the organism and having been lived through for a certain duration (sitting in a cell for a half hour is not the same as sitting in one for a month). It appears, then, that the concept of lived time is a compound of all of the various heterogeneous and more-or-less discontinuous qualitative times formed with the purpose of opposing the concept of homogeneous and continuous quantitative time (clock time).

Even though it is not carried out with rigor, the critique of a public situation organized by official time perspectives should not be undervalued because it points in the direction of consequences of an abstract organizational society that have been ignored by the formalists. From a structural viewpoint, formalism is the symptom of a crisis rather than the most advanced position in life philosophy. Even the most despairing formalists have accepted being thrown back upon the present in the name of intellectual probity or authenticity. Some have even welcomed the advent of creative freedom as a liberation from the bonds of past systems, ignoring the perils of having to reconstitute one's fragmented being in each successive moment. None have looked upon restriction to the present with the scorn with which Basave describes the person who lives in time and for time. The conservative critique shows that there are other aspects of human existence which are under attack in the current era in addition to cultural time perspectives. Not only has there been an explosion of meaning, there has also been an implosion of meaning within personal consciousness. Relativity externally has been accompanied by what Ortega called "intrasubjectivity" and what Unamuno denominated "intraconsciousness" internally. The formalists strip down ordinary conscious experience to its basic structure, which

50

was defined precisely by Korn as a continual opposition between subject and object (liberty and necessity) resolved perpetually and always provisionally in action. However, they remain within the context of meaning, even though they have been driven to the point at which they must initiate a struggle to establish themselves so that they will even be able to entertain a search for meaning. In order to get beyond their position, it is necessary to reject ordinary conscious experience and find some other basis from which to approach the perplexities and tyrannies of our existence.

The bulk of the philosophies of our time, as has been noted above, have been efforts to wed some of the insights of philosophies of immediacy to older philosophies of mediation. Only one body of thought appears to have avoided this move while still rejecting formalism: Henri Bergson's intuitionism. Bergson's analysis revealed strata of time that are inaccessible to ordinary conscious experience (what he called the "practical viewpoint"). However, few twentieth-century philosophers have attempted to use Bergson's analysis as the basis for a life philosophy, perhaps because they were not able to recreate his intuition. The following essay will be an attempt to approach the problem of transpersonal meaning by examining the ways in which meaning is constructed as a mediation out of the polar processes of temporalizing in "intraconsciousness."

II.

The Implosion of Meaning (1)

A new interpretation of human action cannot begin from an analysis of ordinary experience. Everyday life has been reduced by formalists to its minimum structure, relegating transpersonal meanings to the status of myths rather than rationally defensible beliefs. Only a movement of thought turning away from ordinary conscious experience and holding it relative to some "extraordinary" experience can provide an advance over formalism's desperate recreation of the subject and object in each succeeding "specious" present. Such an abnormal or impractical movement of thought, reinterpreting everyday life, was undertaken by Henri Bergson.

The primary significance of Henri Bergson's thought is moral, not metaphysical as he intended it to be in such famous works as *Creative Evolution* and *Matter and Memory*. He devoted these works to the elaboration of his vitalistic interpretation of the absolute. Bergson's original intuition was directed away from the universe and towards the self, which he grasped as a temporalizing process, conceived under the term duration (*durée*). In *Time and Free Will*, Bergson's first major work and the one in which he defines pure duration and opposes it to living in space, temporalizing, or creating time, is not discussed apart from a self process composed of two contrasting directions. Bergson argues that there are two aspects of conscious life, two ways of regarding duration, and two forms of multiplicity: "Below homogeneous duration, which is the extensive symbol of true duration, a close

52

psychological analysis distinguishes a duration whose heterogeneous moments permeate one another; below the numerical multiplicity of conscious states, a qualitative multiplicity; below the self with well-defined states, a self in which *succeeding each other* means *melting* into one another and forming an organic whole."[1]

Bergson remarks that human beings do not normally attend to the deeper levels of the self (those which are more heterogeneous, qualitative, and immediate), because consciousness, "goaded by an insatiable desire to separate, substitutes the symbol for the reality, or perceives the reality only through the symbol." The bases for the insatiable desire to analyze and to abstract are "the requirements of social life in general and language in particular." Yet Bergson did not follow up on his idea that the full range of self experience is kept hidden from consciousness by the "requirements of social life." Had he embellished upon this suggestion, he would have developed a theory in which both the processes of valuation and causation were held relative to those social relations from which they are derived. Instead, he attempted to demonstrate that his intuition of the deeper levels of the self disclosed absolute reality, while the perspective of practical activity merely revealed the survival needs of the individual organism or, as in his *The Two Sources of Morality and Religion,* the social superorganism.

Bergson was led to a metaphysical interpretation of his intuition of duration by the structure of the problem that he was trying to solve. The division of consciousness into two alternative orders, each of which was contradictory to the other, but equally necessary and comprehensive, had been the starting point for modern philosophy since Descartes's scission of thinking substance from extended substance. In Leibniz's hands this division became one between the orders of final and efficient causation, a distinction reflected in Josiah Royce's categories of the world of appreciation and the world of description, and in Alejandro Korn's separation of subject from object and axiology from science (see Chap-

THE IMPLOSION OF MEANING (1)

ter One). The search for harmony between the orders of final and efficient causation had preoccupied modern thinkers up to the formalists who abandoned the quest in favor of urging a strenuous life aimed at establishing creative freedom in each present. Bergson, who attempted to mediate between the two poles of mechanism and finalism (his terms for Liebniz's two orders), was firmly within the modern tradition in the sense that he took for granted the project of unifying opposed perspectives and processes into a meaningful pattern (what was called a cultural time perspective in the preceding chapter). Hence, Bergson's advance over his predecessors was not his particular metaphysical attempt to bind a fractured experience together, which simply added to the "explosion of meaning," but his intuition of the deeper levels of the self that are the very generators of meanings and his suggestion that these levels are usually not accessible because of the requirements of social life.

Leibniz's *Monadology,* written in 1714, contains, in germ, the entire struggle of modern thought to unify the systems of cultural time that had collapsed in the wake of the Middle Ages. Reason can ask two questions about any event: Why did it occur? What purpose does it serve? The answer to the first question is in terms of efficient cause, and that to the second in terms of final cause. Leibniz undertook the effort, repeated by his many successors, including Bergson the metaphysician, to demonstrate that the answers to the two questions were in harmony with one another. While Leibniz acknowledged that "an infinity of slight inclinations and dispositions," each of which was contingent, formed his purposes, he believed that there was a "sufficient or final reason" outside of the "sequence or *series* of this detail of contingencies, however infinite it may be." That final reason was the "necessary substance" that "we call God." Hence, transpersonal meaning was objective for Leibniz because it reposed in God.

Leibniz's thought is worthy of attention because it placed equal stress on the orders of efficient and final causation.

54

THE IMPLOSION OF MEANING (1)

Neither mechanism nor finalism (explanation by ends) was accorded priority or reduced to its opposite, but both were reconciled in God's universal harmony. Leibniz dreamed of inventing a "kind of alphabet of human thoughts" through which everything else could be "discovered and judged."[2] He stated that this dream appeared to him when he was a boy and that "I did not rest until I had penetrated to the root and fiber of each and every theory and reached the principles themselves from which I might with my own power find out everything I could that was relevant."[3] Leibniz did not succeed in inventing the "universal character" that would have allowed him to know the universal harmony with his "own power," but instead bequeathed to his successors the problem and the project.

Kant, who stands at the beginning of German idealism and who is the most influential on the way in which Bergson conceived of his task, translated Leibniz's two orders into "two points of view" from which a rational being "can regard himself, and recognize the laws of the exercise of his faculties, and consequently of all his actions": "*first*, so far as he belongs to the world of sense, he finds himself subject to the laws of nature (heteronomy); *secondly*, as belonging to the intelligible world, under laws which, being independent of nature, have their foundation not in experience but in reason alone."[4] Yet the rational freedom or autonomy, which alone gives human beings meaning, "is only an *idea* (Ideal Conception) of *reason* and its objective reality in itself is doubtful."[5] Hegel's attempt was to show that rational will was not subjective, but the principle of reality. Through his dialectical logic that placed meaning in history, rather than in the subject, he initiated the modern relativistic effort to fulfill Leibniz's dream of the universal character that would harmonize the orders of efficient and final causation.

Bergson inherited Leibniz's problem and project, and retained them for metaphysical purposes in the distinction between mechanism and finalism which he tried to harmonize with such concepts as "creative evolution" and "vital impetus." However, the intuition of duration, rather than presupposing the distinction between the orders of efficient and final causation, both of which, as Korn showed, are components of ordinary conscious experience, presumes a distinction between an "attitude" or "viewpoint" constitutive of "ordinary experience" and one that grasps what might best be called "extraordinary experience." Korn stated that the opposing poles of consciousness are continually synthesized in action and perpetually severed in contemplation. The entire process of conscious experience, comprised by the alternation between action and contemplation and by the two poles of contemplation, must be coordinated into a distinctive attitude that can in turn be opposed to a different one in order for the intuition of deeper levels of the self to be made intelligible. Bergson made just such a distinction between attitudes by contrasting what he called the "practical viewpoint" with that of intuition.

Bergson's Intuition

Bergson defined philosophy as a "conversion of the attention" from the "part of the universe which interests us from a practical viewpoint and *turning it back* toward what serves no practical purpose."[6] He associates the "practical viewpoint" with "normal psychological life," in which there is "a constant effort of the mind to limit its horizon, to turn away from what it has a material interest in not seeing."[7] The principles of the practical viewpoint, the specifications of what Bergson calls "the necessities of action" and of the end or ends to which they are directed, are not made clear by him. Whether the individual strives to dominate the environment or merely to survive, and whether domination or survival refer to the organism primarily or to the group, are questions left without definite answers. However, while Bergson's definition of the practical viewpoint is vague with regard both to its principle and to its object, it includes at least the notions of action directed towards an end, ordinary experience as a limitation

56

upon consciousness, and interests that interpose between attention and virtual experiential contents.

Bergson notes in his essay of 1911, "The Perception of Change," that beginning with the Greeks, Western philosophers have believed that "the discovery of truth demanded a conversion of the mind." The conversion has traditionally consisted of attempting to rise above ordinary experience by "developing other faculties of perception than the senses and consciousness." According to Bergson, Kant rejected this approach of postulating "transcendent faculties," and argued that "if metaphysics is possible, it is through a vision and not through a dialectic." Yet, having "proved that intuition alone would be capable of giving us a metaphysics," Kant stated that such an intuition was impossible, because he believed, along with his predecessors, that "to break away from practical life was to turn one's back upon it."

Bergson believed that rather than to turn one's back upon practical experience, it was necessary to look inside it and to grasp the process of change that composed it. He called this apprehension the intuition of duration or the perception of change. In *Time and Free Will*, Bergson acknowledged the difficulties involved in discussing the *durée*. He noted that if a novelist could tear aside "the cleverly woven curtain of our conventional ego" and reveal "under this juxtaposition of simple states an infinite permeation of a thousand different impressions which have already ceased to exist the instant they are named," that novelist would still have failed to capture the substance of life because the description required words and homogeneous time. Words impose stability when there is none, while homogeneous time, in which events are organized by the clock, transforms the unbroken unity of conscious experience into discrete events, one following the other on a line or ribbon. The best that an artist can do is to "make us suspect the extraordinary and illogical nature of the object" that projects the work and to make us "reflect by giving outward expression to something of that contradiction, that interpenetration, which is the very essence of the elements expressed."[8]

THE IMPLOSION OF MEANING (1)

According to Bergson, the experience revealed by performing the "unnatural act" of "inverting" the practical viewpoint is heterogeneous rather than uniform, qualitative rather than quantitative, dynamic rather than static, continuous rather than discrete, and immediate rather than conceptually mediated. Bergson believed that his intuition had allowed him to "put aside for an instant the veil which we interposed between our consciousness and ourselves." However the notion that reality is ordinarily concealed from human beings presented Bergson with a problem that was to haunt him throughout his philosophical career. If reality is an unbroken temporal process, why is most human existence lived under the form of homogeneous space and spatialized divisible time? If all experiences interpenetrate one another, why do human beings continually mark off and define discrete objects? If consciousness is an intrinsically open and receptive process, why do human beings insist upon an interiority of their own that is inaccessible to others? With regard to ontology, such questions concern the order of priority of such categories as duration and space, and how the practical and spatialized viewpoint is derivable from the intuitive viewpoint. With respect to morality, the questions involve the justification of a being that appears to exist in a fallen state, allowed only momentary and privileged glimpses of reality.

Bergson's response to the questions raised by the need to relate the intuitive and the practical viewpoints was his vitalistic metaphysics. The practical viewpoint was explained functionally as a moment in the evolutionary career of the "impetus of life," constituted by "a need of creation" that is partially blocked by "matter." The vital impetus "seizes upon this matter, which is necessity itself, and strives to introduce into it the largest possible amount of indetermination and liberty."[9] From this description of "creative evolution" it is not far to Korn's dualistic empiricism, in which creative freedom is opposed to necessity in present consciousness, or to Sartre's opposition of *pour soi* and *en soi*, both of which pairs do not presume a unifying vital process that substitutes for the idealist's absolute. Bergson had abandoned the modern relativistic project of defining transpersonal meaning historically, but had not rejected history itself as the vehicle of meaning. The vital impetus is a transpersonal repository of meaning, because it is the process that generates new meanings while fusing them with the old ones in its continuous activity of creation. The vital impetus works through individual human beings, saving their contributions and thereby muting the "tragic sense of life" inherent in the predicament of having to "interpose a veil between our consciousness and ourselves."

In his late work, Bergson turned more towards social philosophy, defining two opposing directions of moral activity in his *The Two Sources of Morality and Religion.* "Closed morality," which is the social expression of the practical viewpoint's limitation on attention, directs the individual's action towards defending the particular group that has provided nurturance and identity. "Open morality," which is the social expression of the intuitive viewpoint's receptivity to experience, is directed towards the formation of an inclusive community in which all human beings would have membership. Again the ground of the discussion is the "vital impulse," but this time the justification of a life directed away from reality is in terms of social functionalism. Bergson argues that there are two models of society in nature: the instinctual society of the ant hill and the bee hive, and the intelligent and quasi-voluntary society of human beings. Only with human beings, Bergson states, has the vital impulse found "the means of continuing its activity through individuals, on whom there has devolved, along with intelligence, the faculty of initiative, independence, and liberty."[10] However, intelligence is not merely a means to group survival, but a possible destroyer of it when used by the individual to avoid social constraints and sacrifices, and to "think only of leading a pleasant life." "Assuming that society is to go on" (an assumption that Bergson, along with other social functionalists, makes), there must be a "counterpoise" to intelligence.

THE IMPLOSION OF MEANING (1)

This counterpoise cannot be instinct, because instinct has been supplanted by intelligence, but can only be "the residue of instinct which survives on the fringe of intelligence." The "virtuality of instinct" is made actual by imagination which counteracts intelligence by creating representations that direct individuals towards discharging their social duties: "This would be the explanation of the myth-making faculty."[11] Closed morality, then, is the result of the evolutionary process of life, and is challenged periodically by charismatic figures who have had a privileged intuition and leap over myths to the vision of a universal humanity. The great founders of religions also have their role within the evolutionary process, which is to spur human beings to transcend their limitations.

Bergson's vitalism is essentially a repudiation of the evidence of his original intuition that experience is, in terms of rational categories, "extraordinary and illogical." Rather than revealing the contradictory and interpenetrating processes that constitute consciousness, such concepts as "creative evolution" and the "vital impetus" are metaphysical notions that form a cultural time perspective which is distinguished from others by its open-endedness, but not by its basis in spatialized, homogeneous time through which life expresses its struggle for indetermination and creative liberty. From the vitalistic perspective, human beings are moments in a series constituted by the process of creative evolution. They must strive to surpass their limitations, but they must not be agonized by the war within them between the practical viewpoint rooted in social convention and myth, and the intuitive viewpoint that grasps indivisible duration. Bergson's career, after completing *Time and Free Will*, was devoted to precisely the project of "turning his back" on the practical viewpoint that he denounced in his predecessors. Through disinterested contemplation, he rose above the conflicts of everyday life and the tensions between the deeper and more conventional levels of the self by showing that they were all necessary in terms of the evolution of the vital impetus. This entire project

THE IMPLOSION OF MEANING (1)

was, of course, a grand exercise in question begging, because Bergson attempted to use tentative and relative evidence from biology to indicate the absolute necessity of certain structures of human life. Not only was his evidence necessarily relative, but it was also a product of the very practical viewpoint that, in terms of his intuition, distorted reality by spatializing it in the service of action.

Bergson's vitalism was a result of the way in which he conceived of his task as a philosopher. He believed that a philosopher should be a metaphysician who could "penetrate into the beyond." He differed from his predecessors, he thought, by realizing that penetrating reality involved a "vision" rather than a special contemplative faculty. Yet in order to elaborate his thought as metaphysics he had to use such categories as the absolute, universality, and necessity, none of which attaches to the intuition of duration itself, but only to one of its possible interpretations. These categories are not even constituents of the practical viewpoint, but are what Kant called "ideas of reason" or "ideal conceptions": idealizations. They have been the staples of rationalist metaphysics which is, in fact, the only possible metaphysics.

Before Bergson took his turn away from intuition and towards idealization, he left important suggestions about the implications of his insight into time. In *Time and Free Will*, he does not associate the more conventional levels of the self with the requirements of the vital impetus, either working against matter or through a social superorganism, but with the actual structure of social relations: "The strangest dreams, in which two images overlie one another and show us at the same time two different persons, who yet make only one, will hardly give us an idea of the interweaving of concepts which goes on when we are awake."[12]

Bergson argues in *Time and Free Will* that recovery of the "fundamental self" depends upon a "vigorous effort of analysis" which "will isolate the fluid inner states from their image, first refracted, then solidified in homogeneous space." The fixed images of what Bergson calls the "conventional ego" are formed from language, which is impersonal, precise, and

THE IMPLOSION OF MEANING (1)

a vehicle for transforming the "confused, ever changing, and inexpressible" contents of experience into "public property." As soon as sensations and tastes are isolated and named, they cease to appear as processes and are presented as discrete objects. While "in reality there are neither identical sensations nor multiple tastes," because duration itself modifies quality, language, which is "the impersonal residue of the impressions felt in a given case by the whole of society," constitutes the inner life as a series of objects that can be manipulated, recalled, projected, and shared. Even the self becomes, in Bergson's terms, "symbolical": an object projected into space, one image among others.

Bergson notes that even "if each of us lived a purely individual life, if there were neither society nor language," consciousness would not grasp pure duration because the idea of a homogeneous space would remain intact. According to Bergson, "the intuition of a homogeneous space" into which objects are projected is a "step towards social life": sociality is, then, inherent in experience. The notion of an external world, which is "the common property of all conscious beings," arises from the same "impulse which leads us to live in common and to speak." Although Bergson does not define the content of this impulse (it was later to become the vital impetus), he shows that "in proportion as the conditions of social life are more completely realized, the current which carries our conscious states from within outwards is strengthened; little by little these states are made into objects or things; they break off not only from one another, but from ourselves."[13] We begin to experience ourselves as instances of feelings that have already been defined and eventually we form a "second self" which "obscures" the first and is "made up of distinct moments, whose states are separated from one another and easily expressed in words."

The drive to rigidify and regiment experience and to make of the self a manipulable image, subject presumably to "behavioral modification," is unexplained by Bergson except in terms of making oneself sharable by "throwing" one's inner life "out into the current of social life." He remarks that

62

the self cannot "withstand the temptation" to introduce into its own life the same distinctions that it makes in the spatialized external world. Only by "deep introspection" is it possible to grasp the original and "fundamental" self, which is constituted by states in a continuous process of becoming. Yet such introspective moments in which we recover ourselves are rare, and for the most part "our life unfolds in space rather than in time; we live for the external world rather than for ourselves; we speak rather than think; we 'are acted' rather than act ourselves."[14]

Bergson's notion, in *Time and Free Will*, that the intuition of duration is associated with the division of the self into conventional or symbolical and what he calls "fundamental" levels, and that the conventional level of the self is a product of social relations, is the essential starting point for reinterpreting his intuition in terms of the problem of meaning, cultural time perspectives, and the processes of temporalization. In the following discussion it will be argued that Bergson's original intuition was not of duration only, but of an entire self process, the form of which is a way of temporalizing, but the content of which is expressing the contents of consciousness unimpeded by the restrictions imposed by social conventions. Opposed to the self process of expression is that of reflection, which is constituted by the objectification of the self into homogeneous time. The interplay between expression and reflection is what is meant by human existence, which takes different attitudes in accordance with the relations between the two processes of temporalizing and experiencing. Interpreting Bergson's intuition as of a self process rather than merely as of duration will allow the social character of what Bergson called the "conventional ego" to be made intelligible.

Expression and Reflection

Ordinary conscious experience, or what Bergson called the practical viewpoint, is a process that alternates between the division of subject from object and their synthesis in action directed towards an end. The present, from this perspective, is, in William James's terms, "specious," because it is merely a vanishing point between what has just occurred and what is about to happen. Time, for the practical viewpoint, is homogeneous and provides the context in which, prospectively, means are chosen for achieving future ends, and, retrospectively, memories are recalled and criticized to consolidate the image of the conventional self. When ends have not been fixed by cultural time perspectives into which the individual's projects can be inserted, the present is filled by the process of choosing among ends or, at the limiting point, of creating them. Whatever diverse aspects the practical viewpoint may reveal, however, it always involves establishing the person as an actor within a historical series, even when the social and cultural implications of activity are not intended by the person but only the consequences for an imagined autobiography. Benedetto Croce writes, "Expression does not possess *means*, because it has not an *end*; it has intuitions of things, but it does not will and is therefore unanalysable into the abstract components of volition, means and end."[15]

The Bergsonian act of "inverting" the practical viewpoint breaks the hold of the "conventional ego" on experience, by dissolving the projects that maintain the self as an image or "persona" extended in homogeneous time. The inversion that leads to the intuition of the deeper levels of the self suspends the motives, the meanings, and the purposes that have sustained action, leaving only the process by which these meanings are assimilated, formed, and created out of experience.

The intuition of the "fundamental" levels of the self reveals that the human being is the center of a conflict between two warring processes, expression and reflection, which are harmonized in ordinary experience by a meaning or goal that limits both of them. The scission of these processes in intuition presumes that the person is no longer principled by a meaning and, therefore, the act of inversion may be called the "implosion of meaning."

64

The processes of expression, the analogue here of Bergson's "fundamental" self, and reflection, the counterpart of his "conventional ego," may be distinguished from one another formally as contrasting and opposing modes of temporalizing, or of creating time. Expression creates or makes the time of the present, while reflection temporalizes the past-present-future. The present of expression is not the same as the "specious" present of ordinary experience which is continually being pulled back into the past or pushed forward into the future. Expression's present is defined by an undivided span of attention into which is injected no preoccupation with a beyond. This present is filled with spontaneous judgments upon whatever contents appear with no concern for the ulterior consequences of these judgments for self-maintenance or for the achievement of goals. Within expression's present are what might be called the "immediate" past and future, denominated so because of their continuous linkage within the actual event through the span of attention. The "last" thought, deed, or feeling, and the "next" one are part of expression's present.

Expression is the process of forming judgments about the particular contents of experience, first by naming them and then by responding to them in such sentimental terms as interesting or boring, tragic or comic, beautiful or ugly. The acts of naming and responding are not separable in the process of expression: fact and value are united in the concrete experience. There is no thought, in the process of expression, that judgments are relative to a subject or to any other context such as social class or nation. Expression inverts the orders of priority embedded in Western philosophy since Plato, endowing judgments of taste with absolute validity and "melting down" (to use Croce's terms) ideas into components of concrete experiences. Expression is volatile, moving explosively from one appearance to the next, forming analogies between realms of experience, such as the physical and the aesthetic, that are usually kept apart in ordinary experience, and disclosing past judgments that were made spontaneously and were later repressed in the service of practical life. Its judgments, though absolute with each present that it forms, may be contradictory over successive presents ranged in homogeneous time, because each spontaneous response is the basis of a perspective that may be conceptually elaborated in the reflective process and thus made exclusive of alternatives. The richness of expression can be judged by the variety of its responses, the number of contradictions, ambivalences, and ambiguities in which it gets entangled, or in Dostoevsky's terms, by its "breadth."

Expression is receptive and appreciative of experience. In this sense Bergson was correct when he characterized the practical viewpoint as one in which consciousness is rigidly limited by the requirements of action and the intuitive viewpoint as one in which no occurrences, however much they might be opposed to efficacious practice, could be excluded from attention. The principle of expression is to assimilate experience, to, in the terms of Max Stirner, "make it one's own" by naming it and taking an attitude towards it. Rather than being prudent and calculating, expression is prophetic and visionary, speaking for a reality that seems to be presented to it instead of being created by it. Expression reveals appreciation to be active rather than passive: experiences must be named to be appreciated; they must be linked to one another by analogy and contrast in order to be identified. Expression, as it appears in intuition, *makes use of* language by personalizing and particularizing it, adjusting sounds to feelings, coining new words, confusing grammatical distinctions. Yet the way in which it makes use of language, by melting it down and personalizing it, suggests that the expressive process is also the origin of language, although it is not sufficient to create a language that distills and impersonalizes experiences, allowing them to be shared.

The prophetic judgments made by expression upon the particular contents of experience are the materials that are formed into life plans and projects by the reflective process, which selects from among them those that can be fit to-

THE IMPLOSION OF MEANING (1)

gether into a relatively coherent image of the self or, in most cases, several overlapping self images. Expression overflows any of the definitions of character that are impressed upon it, because it is not troubled by maintaining experience into a hypothetical time beyond the present and, therefore, evinces a naive courage in facing up to and giving voice to all particulars to which it attends, including those that have been repressed in the practical viewpoint.

Expression is not a self-sufficient process; it is impossible to lead an "expressive life." Expression is not an "analytical" distinction made within a concrete whole; it is an intuited process that appears when the practical viewpoint is inverted. In the alternating dialectic of ordinary experience, expression cannot be distinguished from any other processes because it is dissolved into deliberation and action with respect to systems of meaning attached to cultural or personal time perspectives. Expression's present is revalued and transformed into a stage on the way to some possible future event or as an outcome of some past chain of occurrences. Hence, it is contracted into a "specious" present, a vanishing point.

The counterpart process to expression is reflection, that process in which the subject, "I," or "conventional ego" is created and projected as a stable object into a time perspective of past-present-future. Just as expression's present is not the vanishing present of ordinary experience, reflection's past-present-future is not the extended time perspective of cultural and transpersonal meaning or the personal time perspective shadowed by death. Reflection supervenes over expression's present in order to criticize it in terms of a hypothetical "beyond," some future that cannot be specified concretely, either as immediate or as some event that can be dated, but towards which the individual must be directed. While expression is appreciative and inclusive, reflection is concerned and exclusive. While expression is prophetic, giving voice to what appears, reflection is prudent, expunging and emphasizing particular contents in accordance with

THE IMPLOSION OF MEANING (1)

the destiny it projects for the subject. Reflection's content is a self image which defines the character and projects of the individual and, therefore, the individual's proper responses to events. Reflection uses memory to construct a hypothetical past for the individual, to which emerging experiences are compared and then either accepted into conscious life or rejected and repressed. The selection process does not necessarily evince instrumental or scientific rationality, because reflection's principle is merely transcendence over the present, and the means to such transcendence can be provided by ritual or convention as well as by experiment. Such transcendence also need not involve the will to survive indefinitely, because the self may be interpreted by reflection as part of a group bearing transpersonal meaning or as an entity destined for salvation or for some other form of rebirth. Reflection, as a process of caring for a self in terms of hypothetical pasts and futures, is indifferent to any of the possible dates and meanings that fill the past and future with specific content. The time perspectives of autobiography, history, and myth are forged by expression as prophetic insights and then transformed by reflection into projects that fix a character and a destiny.

Reflection is no more self-sufficient than expression. It is not possible to lead a "reflective life." Neither is reflection an analytical distinction; it is an intuited experiential process resulting from a scission of ordinary experience. When expression and reflection are held apart in intuition a basic tension within consciousness is revealed. The expressive and reflective processes are opposite in direction, the first being receptive and centripetal (assimilating experiences, making them "its own"), and the second being selective and centrifugal (propelling the self out of the present flow of content and into a hypothetical future). Ultimately expression would tend to enclose the entirety of experience in the orbit of the present, transforming the present into eternity and eliminating the "beyond." Ultimately reflection would tend to dissolve itself into an infinite process of negation ending in a

THE IMPLOSION OF MEANING (1)

pure, contentless act. These "ultimates," however, are merely idealizations that are not parts of the intuition, but are mentioned for heuristic purposes and to suggest the roots of contrasting religious conceptions in the dialectical structure of human experience.

The relations between expression and reflection follow the dialectical pattern that Bergson applied to opposing terms throughout his work: the two processes are "at once mutually complementary and mutually antagonistic."[16] They are mutually antagonistic because they divide the human being between the present (immanence) and the past-present-future (transcendence). Yet they are mutually complementary because they combine to form the practical viewpoint, in which the objects and judgments of expression are transformed into the circumstances and goals of action.

Bergson considered the "conventional ego," or what is here called the reflective process, to be closely related to society. The spatialized self image projected into the past-present-future forms the directly experienced basis for idealized "homogeneous time." Bergson argued that the more superficial self is the "spatial and, so to speak, social representation" of the more "fundamental" and inextensible self. He maintained that "our outer and, so to speak, social life is more practically important to us than our inner and individual existence" and, hence, that "an inner life with well distinguished moments and with clearly characterized states will answer better the requirements of social life" than a continual process of becoming, each moment of which is unique. Yet Bergson neither defined the requirements of social life nor did he specify the nature of the relation between reflection and society. His suggestions, however, point in the right direction for discovering the linkages between the two components of the self process and the practical viewpoint of ordinary experience.

Bergson's notion that "the intuition of a homogeneous space is already a step towards social life" contains an important insight into the nature of society. In order to be-

THE IMPLOSION OF MEANING (1)

come a social being one must become part of a larger whole and one must be made relative to others. The vehicle by which the human being is inserted into a wider whole is the self image, through which individuals are juxtaposed in space. The self image provides the person with a distinctive meaning that can be contrasted with the meanings of others. The process of reflection is the form in which the individual is made relative to projects that extend from the past into the future and that involve the actions of others.

Reflection is the inward response to the demand made by others that one be someone in particular, someone giving certain outward responses in specific circumstances. From earliest childhood human beings are provided with definitions of themselves relative to the context set up by adults. One's first meanings are provided by others; one's first self is what C.H. Cooley called the "looking glass self": the reflection of what others have attributed to one. Hence, one's first meanings are extensions of the projects of others: the child *represents* the meanings of significant adults and the child's time is structured by adult perspectives.

It would be a mistake to believe, however, that a self image is merely externally imposed on and implanted in the child, or in any human being, and is then stabilized by the application of social control mechanisms, such as physical coercion and material rewards. In order for a self image to structure activity, it must be *expressed* by the individual: human beings must initially make the definitions and attributions that are given to them their "own"; they must appreciate who they are.

The inherent tension between expression and reflection is evidenced in the child's predicament. The child has more to express and give voice to than any image or attribution can contain. The child demands immediate acknowledgment and attention in a present. Yet the struggle to "socialize" or "civilize" the child involves the withdrawal of acknowledgment and attention by adults. Children are thrown back upon themselves: abandoned in the present, they dwell upon the

70

fear-laden future; reflection (the perspective of past-present-future) is strengthened, the "conventional ego" is stabilized, and the significant adults become ambiguous figures, capable of responding favorably but also capable of ignoring or thwarting. Along with the child's accusation against the other's neglect or abuse goes the emergence of the separate self; the ability to say "you" brings with it the ability to say "I." Yet the content of the "I" is not independent of the attributions that have been provided by others. The child represents the meanings of others by expressing them and acting in terms of them while at the same time becoming individuated and separated from the others through rejecting total dependence upon them. The response to rejection is rejection. The child learns to manipulate, to make others parts of a project, parts of a wider whole. The conventional ego, or reflective process, becomes a permanent source of acknowledgment and attention as the self closes in upon itself. Yet the closure is never perfect: expression demands an other as concrete and inexhaustible as itself, one who can attend to it, acknowledge it, and appreciate it.

The demand for an other as inexhaustible as oneself is the inward counterpart of the external relativity of human beings to one another. This demand is not merely, as it is perhaps for the infant, a demand for physical nurturance and satisfaction, but the expression of a will to be appreciated, to have one's own experience incorporated into and expressed by another, and also to make one's own what the other person has expressed. No "conventional ego," which can only be a pale and partial reflection of some of what has been expressed, is capable of satisfying the will to appreciate and to be appreciated. Yet this demand, which is the social dimension of expression, exists alongside the will to make others predictable parts of a project, to have them complete predetermined meanings attached to the self projected in homogeneous time. The tension between expression and reflection takes the social form of two opposing wills: the will to control others and to realize projects and the will to be appreciated by others and to appreciate them.

THE IMPLOSION OF MEANING (1)

The "practical viewpoint" is an uneasy truce between the antagonistic processes of expression and reflection, which both intertwine with and oppose one another in a multiplicity of ways.Reflection disciplines expression by providing it with a listener in place of another person. Yet at the same time that it individuates the self and separates it from others, reflection also is the bearer of meanings given to the self by others. Expression disciplines reflection by providing it with finite contents. Yet at the same time it disrupts the stability of life plans by the breadth of what it appreciates. Reflection's spatialized image of the self projected in time is the *sine qua non* of sociality, yet its manipulative stance is destructive of society. Expression's ability to appreciate checks rampant manipulation, but stands in the way of programmed cooperation and stable expectations. The practical viewpoint is continually in the process of being constructed out of the tensions between expression and reflection. The only apparent peace arises when human beings are able to adhere to a meaning that they can call their "own" (that they have been able to express) and that can carry them beyond the present and into an indefinite future.

Meaning

The mediation between expression and reflection in ordinary experience is a meaning to be realized by the projection of action into a future. The tensions between the two opposed self processes are, in Bergson's terms, "veiled" in everyday life by a series of actions aimed at realizing finite ends, such as completing a job, cooking a dinner, playing a game, watching a television program, or having a cavity filled. Most of these actions are performed neither spontaneously nor automatically. Usually there must be some deliberation over the appropriate means, some choice among the attitudes, style, or spirit that will characterize the performance, and sometimes doubt about whether the end itself is worth seeking. Often there are conflicts between commitments that cannot be realized simultaneously and frequently

72

there are other conflicts between what appear to be the "authentic" desires of the self and imposed demands, or between what appear to be inclinations stemming from the passions and the imperatives of reason or conscience. Even in ordinary experience, then, the self is pluralized and divided against itself. Yet none of the tensions of ordinary conscious experience destroy the practical viewpoint, constituted by a subject and an object which are synthesized in action. The subject may continually shift, indeed it always does, between the standpoint of authentic vocation striving to overcome acceptance of social norms and the standpoint of social obligation criticizing individual independence, between the view of passionate desire sweeping away convention and the view of conscience suppressing inclination, and between the various conflicting institutional role definitions. However, although subject and object can be instantaneously reversed within and between a multitude of perspectives the structure of the practical viewpoint persists throughout all of these vacillations, even at the limit where the subject adheres to no meaning at all, but derives meaning from the power to entertain and create meanings against an unresponsive world.

The variegated texture of the practical viewpoint is evidence that none of the doctrines about the fundamental content of the conscious self is absolute or necessary. The Kantian notion of a self split between inclination and duty is no more basic than the Orteguian concept of a self split between authentic vocation and submission to social abstractions, or the pragmatic idea of a creative "I" in dialogue with a social "me." Each one of these ideas of the self is a system of meaning that can structure a life by directing activity. The plurality of such perspectives is an index of the explosion of meaning. Each one of the perspectives, including the conflicts or "dialogues" that they involve, can be *expressed* and *appreciated*, and can be taken up by reflection as a self image and projected into a past-present-future. Although the doctrinaire theoreticians of the self may believe

THE IMPLOSION OF MEANING (1)

that they have penetrated to the "deep structures" of human existence, they have merely constructed images of possible subject-object relations, as is evidenced by the ability to live simultaneously under the signs of inclination-duty, authenticity-inauthenticity, and "I"-"me," and even to take either side of any of the pairs at any moment.

For those who have not experienced the explosion of meaning, the conflicts and doubts that pervade everyday life are structured by systems of transpersonal meaning, or cultural time perspectives, that show how the perplexities are necessary in terms of the cosmic time of religions or the historical time of modern evolutionary relativisms. For example, in the Marxist perspective dualisms such as that between authentic vocation and social demands are explained as artifacts of economic exploitation which divides classes against one another and which will be eliminated in a future society principled by the rule "from each according to his abilities, to each according to his needs." The example demonstrates that the function of cultural time perspectives is not to make particular decisions for individuals, but to infuse their private problems with public significance and, thereby, to direct the resolution of those problems towards insertion into the public situation. Hence, it is also incorrect to assume that cultural time perspectives are mere opiates or epiphenomena. They serve to articulate action within a system that transcends the individual's lifetime and thus set limits upon the possibilities that the individual will express. Systems of transpersonal meaning can be transformed into casuistic manuals by organizations exerting coercion, and they can deteriorate into opiates under regimes that blatantly betray their official ideals, but their basic function is to provide a context in which the actions of individuals can be justified by their articulation in a time series. However, the union of cultural time perspectives with the state is inevitable, because the instruments of making and administering policy are the instruments by which the means to salvation are guaranteed and/or by which history is made.

THE IMPLOSION OF MEANING (1)

As cultural time perspectives have increasingly collapsed in the twentieth century, their place has been taken by deliberately administered clock time perspectives of organizations engaged in planning. The hallmark of the present era is not so much planning and programming themselves, because collective projects resulting from self-conscious volition have characterized every civilization, nor is it the principle of economic or instrumental rationality, which has also been present in the past, but the separation of administrative controls from any linkage with systems of cosmic or historical time. The older systems provided a mediation between the perplexities of the individual and action within the public situation, serving to integrate human beings into a community, even when that community was oppressive. Organizational time perspectives, on the contrary, make no reference to individuals as ends, but consider them merely as behavioral organisms held relative to a projected collective result, usually measured statistically and often emphasizing the mere accumulation of means for the organization's continued persistence, such as wealth, power, influence, and loyalty. The principle of contemporary organizations seems to be: Act to serve the needs and desires of individuals and primary groups only to the extent necessary to maintain and/or expand the apparatus. The direction of conglomerate organizations is to become totalitarian, eliminating spontaneity and individuality from the public situation. Such totalitarian tendencies are checked and arrested by the presence of competing conglomerates, the survival of older cultural time perspectives, and, most importantly, by the expressive self process that continually particularizes and overflows abstractions and standardized patterns.

Organizational time perspectives tend to be completely spatialized. Despite the actual limitations posed by the non-spatial expressive process, ideally all relations within the conglomerate structure can be detailed on a chart and defined in a rule book, while all activities can be spelled out in a plan. Planning, especially when it is undertaken over a

THE IMPLOSION OF MEANING (1)

span exceeding a generation, presumes that human beings, some of whom have not yet even been born, can be fit into the prescribed set of activities. Hence, conglomerates attempt to control their "human" environment, first by merely committing their vast resources and thereby structuring options and opportunities, second by making hitherto unorganized groups dependent upon them for facilities, and third by providing self images for the people whom they are attempting to control. The most important control mechanisms, then, do not require the direct manipulation of individuals by means of force or threat, bribery or seduction, fraud, and the mobilization of guilt or shame. Such means of "behavior modification" are brought into play on the margins of control (these margins may be very wide) where the silent controls of resource deployment, dependency relations, and programmed self image fail.

The spatialized time perspectives of conglomerate organizations externalize individuals by conceiving of and treating them as constants and variables within an experimental design. Individuals often experience the organization as a system into which they will be "plugged" in order to perform certain tasks and then pulled out only to be plugged into another set of activities. What is relevant to the organization is not the person's concrete durational being, inwardly expressed as a set of attitudes, dispositions, sentiments, desires, fears, and hopes that are continually mutating in each present, but the person's official biography, composed of the record of the person's involvement with various organizations such as schools, business firms, military services, hospitals, prisons, mental institutions, nursing homes, social service agencies, courts, and other governmental bureaus. Organizations evaluate the person as a threat, a risk, or a prospect, taking appropriate actions in accordance with the judgment; the person tends to evaluate the organization as an obstacle or an opportunity (what Santayana called a "domination" or a "power") with regard to private projects. The basis of relations between conglomerates and the indi-

76

viduals whom they try to organize is mutual exploitation, not mutual aid, although this neo-Hobbesian situation may be blunted by intrusions of traditional forms of consciousness and of outbursts of individuality.

Conglomerates encourage a way of living in cultural time that is the reverse of the form of existence that can be derived from the intuitive viewpoint. The individual's official biography can be internalized and made into a self image that is invested with transpersonal meaning. The individual may then begin to date existence in terms of a "career" or "life cycle" composed of organizationally-defined modules, and to make judgments and evaluations of the self based on organizational notions of achievement. At the extreme of this attitude life is laid out along a homogeneous time line slashed by divisions marking off stages filled by prescribed actions and even by prescribed sentiments, joys, sorrows, and hopes. The individual feels duty bound to have the proper experiences in each module and may feel cheated by missing out on, for example, an adventurous youth or having children at the right time. As opposed to the intuitive viewpoint of a durational being carrying the past continually into the present, the modular perspective makes clean "cuts" between the stages of life. "Retirement," for example, is a new life, an ironical "rebirth" at the end of life, in which the days of work are supposed merely to be memories rather than indelible traces on character, and in which the individual is supposed finally to rest, relax, enjoy, consume the products of the old-age industry, and make some sort of personal peace with the medical establishment and with death.

The modular perspective on life only brings forth and exaggerates the notion that life is insertion into a wider and preexisting whole which is present at the origin of the reflective self (when the child distinguishes an "I" from a "you" and then embarks on existence within a series of ambiguous "we's"), and which is the root of the "conventional ego" and of all cultural time perspectives. The exaggeration stems from the fact that religious and evolutionary systems of transpersonal meaning acknowledged inward perplexities and processes and related them to harmonizing concepts of salvation or temporal perfection: the individual's particularity was "saved" by the older systems, the tensions within the individual's experience were justified. In the modular perspectives of official time, the individual is not a soul or a self, much less a unique durational being, but an *example* of a preexisting pattern. Organizations, particularly the state, find religious and evolutionary time perspectives to be dysfunctional as soon as they have succeeded in making groups dependent upon them for resources and facilities. Organizational plans provide the pattern for the public and spatial disposition of individual actions, while care for the personal meaning of social requirements is assigned to psychologists, psychiatrists, advertisers, "social workers," teachers, and a plethora of "counselors," all of whom are charged with the task of reconciling people to their modules and of certifying their fitness or incapacity to remain in them. These "mind workers," "people workers," or "mental proletarians" apply a variety of homogeneous and modular time perspectives specifying "normal" or "optimal" stages of "development," which supply standards of "goodness of fit" between the individual client, patient, or "ward" and the "roles" which that person is called upon to "play." "Mind workers," who are skilled in taking the *official* role of the other within an existing system of functions, revalue the traditional systems of transpersonal meaning into a "higher functionalism" that acknowledges them as means to "pattern maintenance and tension management" and, hence, limits them to those roles. The "two-dimensional" aspect of traditional and modern relativistic cultural time perspectives must be eliminated by organizations that aspire to plan for the totality of life.

The only concessions that modular perspectives make to the individual's inner life or the more "fundamental" and expressive levels of the self concern the attitudes or emotions with which the person responds to the prescribed stage or phase, and even here efforts at mobilization often try to encourage appropriate enthusiasm and "morale." Organizational systems of transpersonal meaning distinguish between "deviants" who have been improperly socialized and trained, and "normals" who play their roles adequately or even display "excellence" and who accept "transitions" from one stage to another gracefully. Organizations put the individual "on trial" in each new situation by keeping the records up to date and amassing files and evidence that can be used to justify inclusion into or exclusion from opportunity structures. Those who are excluded from active participation in realizing organizational plans, such as prisoners, mental patients, and welfare "cases," are, paradoxically, those whose time is most directly allocated by deliberate decision of hierarchies. The more replaceable actors, who have no specialized skills, are little more autonomous, although they may have a certain "horizontal mobility" and a "private life" that is semi-organized by consumer conglomerates such as the mass media. Specialists and professionals have an added dimension of "vertical mobility" programmed into modules extended along a career line. Only the directors of the conglomerates, the so-called "power elites," exist in an environment filled with surprises and unique occurrences, because they are in charge of the unresolved conflicts between organizations and the efforts to mobilize and control emerging groups. They have genuine biographies as durational beings and make official history rather than suffer, bear, and receive it. Not only do they have a career pattern; they also have a qualitative mobility that allows them to move between different *kinds* of organizations, such as the superstate, the multinational corporation, and the multiversity.

Modular time perspectives break the link between the individual's particular existence as a concrete durational being expressing meanings and then projecting them into a past-present-future and the transpersonal domain of a public situation. The conglomerates organize the public situation and define the modules into which people will be fit, but

THE IMPLOSION OF MEANING (1)

beyond the provision of "organic solidarity" hierarchically imposed they have no concern for the person. This neglect can be alternatively interpreted as a gift of freedom that allows each individual to work out a personal meaning for life and death. Alongside the official time perspectives of organizations appears the uniquely personal time perspective of the individual, which is shadowed by death, the one event that defies modular interpretation, even if it has been successfully organized.

The collapse of cultural time perspectives and their substitution by the official time of organizations has had the consequence of intensifying individuation and personal time. Modular life plans, programmed by organizations, make what Bergson called the "conventional ego" even more externalized, spatialized, and conventionalized (stylized) than it was when the person's perplexities were fused with cosmic or historical time series. Existentialism, particularly those forms of it concerned with death, "nothingness," and rehabilitation of inward experiences, is not an accidental or transient life philosophy associated with specific historical cataclysms, but the dialectical counterpart or twin of organizational functionalism, which declares meaning to be an instrument of pattern maintenance and tension management: a safety valve for "emotions" that have not yet been disciplined and controlled by administration. What Edward Tiryakian called the opposition between "sociologism" (exemplified by Durkheim) and "existentialism" is the split that increasingly structures human existence in an organizational society. From the viewpoint of sociologism, existentialism represents the anarchistic protest of the "deviant" who has not been adequately socialized, while from the standpoint of existentialism, sociologism is the quintessence of "inauthenticity": the denial of the human search for a meaning, for the salvation of one's contributions, for the acknowledgment that one is irreplaceable, intransferable, unique, in a word, important.

The existentialists, beginning with their "precursors" such as Dostoevsky, discovered that time takes on a new quality

80

for a person whose life is not in some way extended trans-personally beyond physical death by a system of meaning. The collapse of cultural time perspectives leads to what the Mexican philosopher Basave calls "living in time and for time." The personal time perspective shadowed by death appears in a context in which the individual's particularity, that which cannot be exhausted by a social function, has no value beyond what it is worth for that individual and for specific others who might appreciate it. The person who is unwilling or unable to be absorbed into the modular time perspectives of organizations falls back into either one of two broad forms of life: utilitarianism or existentialism, the con-temporary equivalents of Epicureanism and stoicism, both of which were also the products of the collapse of received systems of transpersonal meaning.

Utilitarianism, far and away the most commonly adopted option, makes living in time and for time a quest for socially available values such as consumer goods or for the extrinsic organizational values, reflective of self esteem *(amour pro-pre),* such as wealth, power, influence, or authority. The utilitarian life, unlike the Epicurean, is not one of repose and adaptation to the flux of matter, but one of agitation and expectancy. For the utilitarian the lesson of death is that no moment of life should escape from the self and be delivered over to anyone or anything else. The standard for what is useful derives, as Rousseau clearly saw in *Emile,* from social valuations. Hence, the utilitarian emphasizes the conven-tional ego and reflects in microcosm the principles of con-glomerate organizations, with the difference that these val-ues are appropriated for the purposes of self realization: the utilitarian responds to the conglomerate's exploitation of individuals by attempting to exploit the conglomerate. Often this relation of mutual exploitation is not antagonistic, but works to the enhancement of both parties. Yet there is a quality of desperation to the utilitarian life that alternates with boredom. The individual is off balance, striving to establish and maintain an advantageous position, and in moments of slack time becomes impatient and bored.

THE IMPLOSION OF MEANING (1)

Existentialism makes living in time and for time a rebellion against organizational determination and definition. The lesson of death for the existentialist is that individuals are responsible for their actions, that they will not be saved by any transcendent person or by any historical dynamic, but that whatever value appears in the public situation is their creation. Unlike the stoic, whose strict life was justified by universal reason, the existentialist has no grounds but acceptance of freedom for the harsh struggle to achieve and maintain authentic choosing. The existentialist's life is no less desperate than the utilitarian's, but the desperation is a product of the necessity of reviving one's freedom and responsibility in each successive vanishing present in full awareness that past commitments can be revoked, that nothing is necessary or essential, that every deed is a determination of the self to be criticized and transcended in the next present, that authenticity itself exists only in the "specious" present, and that the most oppressive object that the subject confronts is the objectification of the past moment's subject. The existentialist, no less than the utilitarian, is unwilling to deliver the self to anyone or anything other than the self. In Kierkegaard's terms, the "self is a relation to itself." For the utilitarian there must be no alienation from "having," while for the existentialist there must be no alienation from "doing."

The time perspective of a personal life that is not articulated with respect to some transpersonal system of meaning tends, under the shadow of death, to collapse into the present; not the present of expression, but the "specious" present of the minimal practical viewpoint. Ortega defined "otherness" (*alteracion*) and "in-oneselfness" (*ensimismamiento*) as the two poles between which "intra-subjectivity" vacillates. The utilitarian seizes upon otherness and lives to amass socially available values, while the existentialist seizes upon "in-oneselfness" and lives to claim and reclaim freedom. The utilitarian is threatened from without by organizations and others who are engaged in a ceaseless search for power after power, while the existentialist is threatened

THE IMPLOSION OF MEANING (1)

from within by self-produced objectifications. Both lives contain distinctive blends of expression and reflection. Utilitarians express themselves through making socially available values their "own" and reflect themselves by carrying over a self image compounded from these values from one present to the next. Existentialists express themselves through their negation of definitions that are in the process of becoming their own and reflect themselves through carrying that negation into the future as a pursuit of authentic choosing. Hence, neither form of personal life represents either of the two self processes to the exclusion of the other, although the utilitarian tends towards the limit of expression and the existentialist towards the limit of reflection.

At the margins between personal time perspectives devoid of transpersonal significance and the intuitive inversion of the "practical viewpoint" are two unattainable and contradictory ideals between which conscious life vacillates and which structure its perplexities and dilemmas. When the utilitarian life loses its anchor in social values, it collapses into the ideal of "ownness," while when the existentialist life loses its ground in rebellion, it collapses into the hunger for immortality.

The categories that are used in life philosophy, and here only philosophies of human life (philosophies of conduct, of civilization, and philosophical anthropologies) are meant, originate in the experience of human beings: what Unamuno called "men of flesh and bone." Most life philosophies address perplexities, difficulties, or problems that their creators could not resolve with the meanings that their cultures made available to them. They are attempts to reconstruct the practical viewpoint on a new basis by reordering tables of values and by conceiving of new oppositions and harmonies within experience. The previous discussion shows that the structure of a life philosophy is some synthesis of the processes of expression and reflection, even though the majority of life philosophers have not proceeded from the basis of intuition and have not necessarily acknowledged the self

THE IMPLOSION OF MEANING (1)

processes that constitute conscious experience. Most life philosophers have created perspectives that can be made the foundations of an actual existence because they have managed to include both poles of the tension within experience in their views. A small minority has followed a different path. Using what Bergson called the method of "analysis and recomposition," they have taken a single fragment of experience and have idealized it as a concept, then turned back to experience with the aim of interpreting it solely in terms of that concept. Such philosophers have found it necessary to embrace a contradictory view of existence, because the basic tension in experience inevitably builds contradiction into any effort to construct a unilateral view. The philosophers of contradiction come as close to the intuitive viewpoint as it is possible for a speculative method to approach, because the fragments upon which they seize are the manifestations of the two self processes that appear when the practical viewpoint begins to unravel or dissolve in consciousness.

The philosophers of contradiction are extreme individualists who have reduced their experience to either utilitarianism or existentialism. They have taken one or the other of these perspectives to the vanishing point of the "specious" present and have made an effort to grasp the flux itself and make it into the principle of life. For the extreme utilitarian the flux appears as "having" or "using," while for the extreme existentialist it appears as "doing" or "transcending." The great philosophers of contradiction in the modern era are Max Stirner, whose ultra-utilitarianism is expressed in the concept of "ownness," and Miguel de Unamuno, whose ultra-existentialism is reflected in his idea of the "hunger for immortality." Proceeding from two entirely different bases, they reach similar conclusions about a life shorn of all transpersonal meaning.

Stirner's philosophy is based on the militant effort to rid himself of "possessions" so that he can be his "own." To be possessed is to live for something alien to oneself, to split

84

oneself between an ideal self image that one has not and that, perhaps, one cannot realize, and an actual self which is held in contempt and scorn. To be one's own is to accept oneself completely, to abolish any tension in one's existence by realizing fully that all conflict between duty and inclination, authentic self and actual self, individual self and social self can be dissolved by an act of affirmation. What one can assimilate and express spontaneously is one's own; what one must strive to achieve possesses one and must be gotten "rid of." The process of becoming one's own is, paradoxically, the farthest thing from spontaneous; it is a ruthless discipline: "We must first come down to the most ragamuffin-like, most poverty-stricken condition if we want to arrive at *ownness*, for we must strip off everything alien."[17] One must, then, be *possessed by ownness* in order to become one's own. Stirner comments that "nothing seems more ragamuffin-like than naked-Man," but then adds that even the idea of human nature or essence must be discarded in order to confront oneself as a unique individual (Unamuno would later say that each person is a "unique species"). Once the last "rag," the idea of human essence, has "fallen off," the "ragamuffin has been stripped of ragamuffinhood itself, and therewith has ceased to be what he was, a ragamuffin." And then in a stunning reversal, marked by a pause, Stirner returns to declare: "I am no longer a ragamuffin but have been one."[18]

Stirner's major work, *The Ego and His Own,* is divided into two sections, the first of which details his process of getting rid of all possessions and the second of which is a description of how he possesses himself. He criticizes all alienations, not only every system of transpersonal meaning, but also living to distinguish oneself from others (he claims to be *unique,* not *special*) and to accumulate possessions (he states that one should get rid of material objects that are disagreeable). After his merciless self criticism, he is left merely with himself, "having," and "using." It is here that his philosophy and, presumably, his life fall into deep contradiction.

THE IMPLOSION OF MEANING (1)

Stirner claims to possess himself, to be his "own," but when he attempts to define himself, to seize himself and to appropriate himself, he finds that he is a "creative nothing." "Ownness" turns out to be inseparable from "possession." Self ownership implies for Stirner the ability to get rid of any object, whether it be material or ideal. Yet there is no self in the absence of a self image, or what Dostoevsky called a "stable meaning." The "creative nothing," then, produces objects that in turn must be gotten rid of: "ownness" is a momentary vanishing point in the specious present. One is never one's own, but is continually being possessed by ownness. The notion of being one's own is the ideal of expression, which is perpetually assimilating the contents of experience. However, in order for expression to persist from one present to the next, it must despoil reflection of any specific content and use it for its own purposes. Reflection, which is the root of possession, exacts the toll of making expression itself into an ideal to be projected into the past-present-future and imposes a ruthless discipline that reduces the person continually to a naked "ragamuffin." Extreme utilitarianism involves the project of *using and possessing* reflection as an instrument of expression. Yet the very necessity of expressing "ownness" in terms of a project shows that it is a contradictory concept representing a contradictory life.

The impossibility of one part of the self process gaining total domination over the other is evidenced by the cruel and pitiless ethic that Stirner is impelled to adopt. There turn out to be limits to what can be assimilated and made one's own. In the second part of his work, Stirner contrasts ownness not with possession, but with piety. He criticizes any sacrifices to others, not merely to ideas, as instances of weakness and sets up an ideal of selfishness rather than of ownness. Anticipating Nietzsche, he identifies unselfishness with weakness: "But the weak, as we have long known, are the—unselfish. For them, for these its weak members, the family cares, because they *belong* to the family, do not belong to themselves and care for themselves."[19] Here to be one's

THE IMPLOSION OF MEANING (1)

own does not mean to be able to assimilate and express the contents of experience, but to be strong enough to get rid of the other person. Life becomes a struggle in pursuit of an authenticity defined as the possibility of absolute independence, not conceived, to be fair to Stirner, as a live option, but as something even worse: a regulative *ideal.* The unique one has been transformed into the strong one. Those who are weak are inauthentic; they should be passed over. One's own weakness, indeed, should be expunged and passed over. Reflection has at last won the struggle with expression, binding it to a strenuous quest for self perfection, the very quest that "ownness" was supposed to eliminate.

Unamuno, the ultra-existentialist, acknowledged that his philosophy of life, which is most fully expressed in his *Tragic Sense of Life,* was based on contradiction. As much as Stirner, Unamuno was preoccupied with himself; however, he was not concerned with possessing or owning himself, but with perpetuating himself infinitely. All of Unamuno's thought turns on his attempts to satisfy his hunger for immortality, which he cannot still by adhering to any systems of transpersonal meaning, because none of them promise to save him as a "man of flesh and bone," who was born at a particular date and has particular interests, passions, and relations. Unamuno's philosophy exemplifies the attempt to make reflection, the process of propelling a self into the future, dominant over expression.

The counterparts of ownness and possession for Unamuno are what he calls the "individual" and the "person." Like *The Ego and His Own, The Tragic Sense of Life* is a spiritual autobiography. It details Unamuno's struggles to sacrifice the individual to the person and his successive failures. He defines the individual as the principle of preservation (continuance of the physical presence) and the person as the principle of perpetuation (continuance of the self image in others, in history, or in God's mind): "I do not want to die—no; I neither want to die nor do I want to want to die; I want to live forever and ever and ever. I want this "I" to live—this poor "I" that I am and that I feel myself to be here and now, and therefore the problem of the duration of my soul, of my own soul, tortures me."[20]

The deepest problem for Unamuno is not the conflict between reason and faith in resurrection of the flesh, which he uses to structure his agony, but his doubt that there is even a self to be saved. He claims that he wants "all or nothing" (*todo o nada*), meaning that he wants no substitute for physical immortality, but then adds cryptically that he wants "*all and nothing.*" In his discussion about "the bottom of the abyss," he claims to become dizzy and nauseous when he attempts to think of himself as not existing. Yet when he attempts to define himself, he finds that all objectifications slip away from him. The person, which is a principle of "continuity" when considered passively, is open to experience and continually in flux. If it could not assimilate more and more experience, it would disappear. Yet were it to assimilate everything, it would also dissolve, because there would be no more contrast between itself and anything else: time would have been swamped in eternity. The individual, which is a principle of "unity" when considered passively, limits the person, but is a mere container, devoid of content. What remains of the self, upon analysis, is only an image in perpetual mutuation.

Unamuno finds that when he has made all of his particular characteristics contingent he is, no less than Stirner, a "creative nothing." When he reaches the "summit of tragedy" and acknowledges that salvation can only be achieved by sacrificing the individual to the person, by "the sacrifice of our own individual consciousness upon the altar of the perfected Human Consciousness, of the Divine Consciousness," he suddenly reverses himself and rebels, demanding "an eternal purgatory, then, rather than a heaven of glory; an eternal ascent."[21] He demands infinite time and "a substratum of doubt" so that whatever he is at any moment, he can always desire to be something else.

Unamuno's tragedy is the necessary defeat of reflection

THE IMPLOSION OF MEANING (1)

when it is made into a life principle. Reflection is nothing but the process of projection into time. It needs a particular and finite content to project, or it dissolves into nothing. Yet it also disappears if the content remains fixed, because as Bergson pointed out, duration itself is not an abstract idea, but an element of qualitative change. There is no fixed self for reflection to project, only an image that necessarily falsifies changing experience, that is just an idea, a "conventional ego" that Unamuno himself admits is a social product which exists only insofar as there are social relations.[22] The dynamic of Unamuno's life reverses that of Stirner's: the first is perpetually in the process of creating a self image that can be saved by reflection, while the second is continually in the process of destroying a self image so that it can be "melted down" into expression. The bare hunger for immortality is checked by the opposing hunger to be someone in particular here and now, just as self ownership is checked by the hunger to carry it into the future. Unamuno not only fears a final death; he also trembles before the death and rebirth of himself in each present. With no fixed meaning to continue, he is left with the contradictory project of continuing nothing but the will to continue.

The perpetual destruction and construction of the self in successive "specious" presents is the result of the implosion of meaning just as it was the consequence of the explosion of meaning. From either direction the practical viewpoint collapses into a war between opposing and irreconcilable processes. Neither the implosion nor the explosion of meaning are experiences that every human being must or should undergo. The preceding discussion has not been an attempt to institute a new doctrine of authentic existence, calling upon people either to, in Dostoevsky's words, "lacerate themselves" or to revive belief in some cultural time perspective. It has been, rather, an exercise in description and clarification of what can happen and seemingly has happened to some of the more sensitive human beings who have tried to achieve self knowledge in the modern era. As such, it reveals the base point to which modern conscious-ness can be reduced. Those who have touched this base point in their own lives have experienced what it means to stake one's entire existence on ideas and then to find that there are no ideas that can satisfy them. A turning away from meaning as the center of one's existence demands a refusal to regard creation as the defining mark of the self.

III.

The Implosion of Meaning (2)

The modern struggle for transpersonal meaning, for a cultural time perspective in which to insert one's life and work, reaches its climax in the effort to exhaust each available system and, finally, to create a new perspective that can integrate the totality of human existence. Formalism confronted the explosion of meaning by abstracting from each particular system the structure of conscious activity, leaving each individual in the "specious" present. Bergson's intuitionism imploded meaning, revealing the mutually antagonistic and complementary processes that make up the practical viewpoint, but similarly left human beings without a context into which to project themselves. Those who experienced the collapse of cultural time perspectives in their own lives remained in relation to a public situation, although they could not define it with certainty. Even those who chose a life of resistance and rebellion had to resist and rebel against something in particular. Lacking any focus for action to which they could commit themselves without reservation, each of the traditional and modern systems appeared to them as hypotheses which they could test in their own lives by appealing to the "will to believe": "As a child, then, I had almost fallen into the well. When grown up, I nearly fell into the word 'eternity,' and into quite a number of other words too—'love,' 'hope,' 'country,' 'God.' As each word was conquered and left behind, I had the feeling that I had escaped a danger and made some progress. But no, I was only changing words and calling it deliverance."[1]

90

THE IMPLOSION OF MEANING (2)

Nikos Kazantzakis exemplifies, perhaps better than any other twentieth-century thinker, the vicissitudes of a life led in search of meaning by someone who cannot believe in the truth of any cultural time perspective. Kazantzakis's quest for meaning was motivated by the need he felt for deliverance from the struggle within his being between what he called "the spirit and the flesh." He observes in his prologue to *The Last Temptation of Christ* that "my principal anguish and the source of all my joys and sorrows from my youth onward has been the incessant, merciless battle between the spirit and the flesh."[2] By these two terms Kazantzakis refers to what Unamuno called the "person" and the "individual": the principle of continuity with and perpetuation through others, and the principle of unity within and preservation of oneself. Unamuno's *Tragic Sense of Life* is a spiritual autobiography recounting his efforts to sacrifice the individual to the person and the continual reassertion of the individual at the end of each trial. Kazantzakis's spiritual autobiography, *Report to Greco,* follows the same pattern, with the difference that Unamuno's hunger for immortality is replaced by the need for deliverance.

Kazantzakis sought deliverance not only in traditional religious perspectives, but also in the modern relativistic systems, such as Marxism and nationalism. He did not interpret these systems as theories that could be proven true or false according to rational standards, but as premises for action that could be made to come true if enough people were dedicated to their realization and sacrificed themselves for the vision. Hence, he transformed all deterministic theories, whether materialist or idealist, into what William James called "live options" for commitment. In his transition between Buddhism and his awakening to Marxism, Kazantzakis notes that he saw "how creative man's intervention is, and how great his responsibility": "We are all to blame if reality does not take the form we desire. Whatever we have not desired with sufficient strength, that we call nonexistent."[3]

Yet Kazantzakis was never either willing or able to seize

upon one of the live options and devote himself to it, and thereby to gain deliverance from his anguish. While visiting Soviet Russia, he lost his exuberance for the class struggle and reached the realization that life is not sacrifice, but agony: "Gradually I began to understand that it does not matter very much what problem, whether big or small, is tormenting us; the only thing that matters is that we be tormented, that we find a ground for being tormented."[4] Each of Kazantzakis's efforts to deliver himself to a system of transpersonal meaning ends with the same failure and with the same reassertion of the agonized individual, the "underground man" who demands the "freedom to be free" and the right to suffer as a particular being who cannot be exhausted by any system.

Kazantzakis's thought continually vacillates between the poles of individual and person. When he is trying to gain deliverance by sacrificing the individual to the person, the flesh to the spirit, he declares: "Learn to obey. Only he who obeys a rhythm superior to his own is free."[5] When he is at the end of each trial he reverses himself and speaks of systems of meaning as "gumdrops" and "cowardly consolations" that are "good for dotards, weaklings, and vegetarians."[6] Deliverance, for Kazantzakis, would have meant a harmony between the spirit and the flesh, a reconciliation between "these two primordial forces which are so contrary to each other." Yet in the terms of his predicament such a harmony was impossible, because living according to any system of transpersonal meaning is a sacrifice of the flesh to the spirit, while repudiating such systems is a sacrifice of the spirit to the flesh.

The polar opposition between the two "forces," spirit and flesh, is the most overtly manifest and, in Bergson's terms, "conventionalized" appearance of the ideals of immortality and ownness, and, on a deeper level, of the reflective and expressive processes. Spirit is guided by the insight that "man is not immortal, but rather serves Something or Someone that is immortal." One realizes spirit by delivering oneself

THE IMPLOSION OF MEANING (2)

to what Kazantzakis calls the "Cry of the times": that project which has spontaneously captured masses of people and to which each will be sacrificed. The individual's relation to the Cry should be voluntary submission and cooperation: the reflective process should project the person into history. Flesh is guided by the love of particular and present existence, expressed by Kazantzakis's alter ego, Zorba the Greek, as a process of getting rid of possessions and of becoming one's own: "Rescued from my country, from priests, and from money. I began sifting things, sifting more and more things out. I lighten my burden that way. I—how shall I put it?—I find my own deliverance, I become a man."[7]

Hence, the process of submitting to systems of transpersonal meaning (for Kazantzakis they included Christianity, Buddhism, Greek nationalism, Nietzsche's eternal recurrence, and Marxism-Leninism) is balanced by the process of dispossessing oneself of them and sifting out everything but one's own power to express within a present. To find one's own deliverance is, in Stirner's terms, to be a "unique one," to be one's own. To submit to the "Cry" is to transcend oneself in pursuit of an immortality that will eliminate one's individual being. One becomes, in Kazantzakis's words, a "savior of God," not of oneself.

The successive alternations of Kazantzakis's life between ownness and the hunger for immortality give his existence the form of modular time. His modules, however, are not stages within a preordained system of meaning, but different meaning systems, each of which define their own phases of development; he did not live within a single system of cultural time, but within several of them serially. Kazantzakis interpreted each cultural time perspective as a new trial. He was reborn in each one, having discarded the last as a "cowardly consolation." In search of deliverance, he did not treat himself as a durational being, changing irrevocably and uniquely as the result of each successive experiment, but as a mass of flesh or matter to be remolded anew each time by the discipline which he imposed upon himself. He interpreted

THE IMPLOSION OF MEANING (2)

each system of meaning primarily as an ascetic method through which his love of particular and present existence could be transmuted or refined into a gift of spirit or something greater than himself. He judged, then, his success or failure in terms of whether the flesh rebelled against his act of sacrifice and deliverance—and it always did.

No master, whether Christ, Buddha, Nietzsche, Lenin, or Odysseus, could prove equal to Kazantzakis's contradictory demands. He was either unwilling or unable to perform the one act that would have given him deliverance: to submit himself to the *truth* of any system of meaning, to believe that a particular table of values defined human nature, to humble himself enough to exercise faith. Despite the variegated pattern of his successive projects, the essential structure of his life remained the same. It was an agonized, tormented, and contradictory struggle to sacrifice himself while maintaining his independence of will, to treat each one of his commitments as relative to himself rather than to treat himself as relative to a commitment. The contradiction between sacrifice and experiment assured that Kazantzakis would always be able to transcend his masters and achieve superiority over them by passing them over. One might picture him as an incarnation of Hegel's absolute spirit, passing through each moment of spiritual evolution, not only dialectically, but concretely, and then gazing over all of them with the superiority gained by exhausting their possibilities.

> The human being cannot support absolute freedom; such freedom leads him to chaos. If it were possible for a man to be born with absolute freedom, his first duty if he wished to be of some use on earth would be to circumscribe that freedom.[8]
>
> I had been struggling for a lifetime to stretch my mind until it creaked at the breaking point in order to bring forth a great idea able to give a new meaning to life, a new meaning to death, and comfort to men.[9]

The only terms upon which Kazantzakis would have consented to become a savior of God rather than of himself

THE IMPLOSION OF MEANING (2)

would have been his own. Had he been able to create a "great idea" to which others gave their allegiance, he then would have been loyal to that idea. However, despite his acknowledgement that freedom to entertain diverse and contradictory meanings is insupportable, he refused to give up that freedom. He directed himself towards the goal of "bringing forth a great idea," but the only idea that he was able to generate was an expression of his project. Confronting as completely as any thinker the explosion of meaning and its attendant possibility of imaginatively crossing social, cultural, and historical boundaries, he did not create his own meaning, but sublimated all previous meanings to a mythical and poetic dimension. He transformed Marxism, for example, into a myth of collective ascension of the spirit over matter through bloody historical action rather than traditional disciplines of individual self perfection. He made of Nietzsche a martyr to eternal recurrence. He made of his Christ a model of himself: a struggler trying to overcome the flesh and always on the verge of succumbing to temptation. Kazantzakis attempted to make each meaning system, each prophet, his own. He did not transcend them by giving a *new* meaning to life and death, but by making them relative to himself and to one another. He did not give comfort to human beings, but left as his legacy an example of torment and agony.

Each system of meaning ended by being, for Kazantzakis, a mask behind which he expressed himself. He would get rid of the mask as soon as he had exhausted the part or had become bored or disgusted with it. Although he continually claimed to be submitting himself to the disciplines of others, he actually submitted them to his own primarily aesthetic standards, judging them by their ability to give him insights into himself and by their effectiveness in stirring his enthusiasm and action. It is indicative of his project that he could not accept the moral perfection of Christ, but embraced the heresy that Christ succumbed to temptation. He was an heir of Descartes, accepting nothing that did not fit his own measure, although he attempted to make his measure as

THE IMPLOSION OF MEANING (2)

generous as possible and did not define it in terms of reason, but in terms of spirit and quality.

Kazantzakis's own myth was a poetical embroidery of formalist categories, a mixture of Royce's absolute and Camus's absurd. He symbolized the object of his efforts at deliverance as the "Struggler," a force at work in the universe shaping and forming matter and directing it towards an ultimate end that could not be known by human beings. Depending upon where he was in his continual vacillation between spirit and flesh, he would interpret the Struggler alternatively as an effort to spiritualize the universe demanding the cooperation of human beings (the absolute shorn of predestination) or as a dynamism completely indifferent to and exploitative of human will and desire (the absurd personified). Kazantzakis interpreted his own life as a desperate attempt to insert himself into the Struggler's enigmatic project, sometimes as an enthusiastic and freely committed comrade in arms and sometimes as a resigned slave or tool. The Struggler was made manifest in history and, so, Kazantzakis sought to deliver himself through discerning its "cry" or project and then dedicating himself to it.

Kazantzakis faced the paradox of having to create the Struggler's project simultaneously with serving it. He noted that each era has its own "cry," peculiar to itself, and that the Struggler was in perpetual mutation. If each one should be a savior of God, each one must also invent God and must refuse to submit to prior definitions. The absurd absolute does not provide the comfort of Royce's absolute, which offered individuals the assurance that their strivings were integral components of the final completed meaning. Rather, belief in the Struggler is no more than belief in one's own powers to create within a specious present.

Kazantzakis acknowledged the implications of his contradictory cultural time perspective. He argued, in Hegelian fashion, that "we live in our epoch and consequently do not see it," but added that because transcendence is a creative act nothing is "assured beforehand," and that the "future

THE IMPLOSION OF MEANING (2)

may be a total catastrophe; it may be a pusillanimous compromise."[10] He concluded that our "duty" is "to carefully distinguish the historic moment in which we live and to consciously assign our small energies to a specific battlefield."[11] Yet he was similar to such formalists as Mannheim and Ortega, both of whom also defined the self as a vocation with reference to historical circumstances. He could not discharge the duty of assigning his energies to anything specific, but devoted himself to the metaproject of defining the conditions for deliverance which he could not meet. Despite the breadth of his generosity and awareness, Kazantzakis was no different from spare and analytical thinkers such as Camus and Korn who seized directly upon the insight that the self must be recreated anew in each present through a process of opposing subject to object.

The conclusion of Kazantzakis's quest for deliverance was to abandon the search altogether in favor of his own peculiar variant of formalism: the Cretan glance. Through the vehicle of Odysseus, yet another mask, he proclaims that he has been "delivered from deliverance." He declares that "time, as though changed into eternity, seems to have stopped." In his final reflections Kazantzakis is willing to accept living within the specious present, shorn of any cultural time perspectives. He declares that the only human value is to live and die bravely, "without condescending to accept any recompense" and with "joy, pride, and manly courage" in the face of "the certainty that no recompense exists." The Cretan glance, the approach to life "without hope and fear but also without insolence," poetizes the absurd revolt of the self perpetually in process between creation and destruction. Yet even in his act of resignation Kazantzakis cannot or will not abandon the agony that marked his experiments in meaning. He manipulates the mask of Odysseus, admitting that he "created" it and then leaps from existentialism to the will to believe, announcing that Odysseus, the exemplar of the Cretan glance, "was the charm that would lure the tenebrous and luminous forces that create the future": "Faith moves mountains; believe in him and he would come."[12] Hence, even at the end of his quest Kazantzakis could not abandon reflection in favor of expression. He made delivery from deliverance into an idea that could be projected into the past-present-future and so provide deliverance itself.

Although it might appear so from a superficial examination of his vacillations and contradictions, Kazantzakis was not a "passive eclectic," a dilettante, or an asystematic and undisciplined thinker. He cannot be dismissed as a "poet" who transformed theories of truth into aesthetic visions and who, therefore, does not deserve the attention of serious philosophers. While it is indisputable that Kazantzakis employed aesthetic categories primarily, his purpose was not to transform philosophies into works of art, but to make them express the structure of his existence. He found that he could not make a system of meaning his own until he endowed it with emotional quality: theories had to be made visions if they were to be worthy of loyalty and commitment. Kazantzakis also had a human ontology based upon the polarity between spirit and flesh, which, in Bergsonian terms (he studied under Bergson), he related in a dialectic of mutual antagonism and mutual complementarity. The structure of his thought, though formally contradictory, mirrors the tensions between expression and reflection in a multitude of ways and appears to be asystematic only because of its complexity. Contradiction is not a fault when there is more than one voice speaking through the person, and Kazantzakis had many voices. Vacillation is not a fault when it stems from the powerful attraction of opposing ideals rather than from weakness of will.

Kazantzakis's work reveals the multiple forms in which the tensions between expression and reflection are made manifest in a practical viewpoint divested of stable transpersonal meaning. The distinctive structure of a life uncommitted to a single cultural time perspective is alternation between opposing poles of experience, or what Hispanic philosophers call the *zozobra*. Variations on the *zozobra* appear in such writers as Unamuno who alternated between the "individual"

THE IMPLOSION OF MEANING (2)

and the "person," Dostoevsky who jumped between individual rebellion and communal solidarity (the Grand Inquisitor and Father Zossima), and Kafka who leaped between eternal permanence and temporal impatience. There are many variants of the *zozobra* in Kazantzakis's thought, all of them revolving around the basic disjunction between freedom and deliverance.

Freedom and deliverance are each compounds of expression and reflection. Freedom is reflective in that it refers to the ability of human beings to project themselves into a past-present-future in accordance with one out of many possible meanings. Yet it is expressive, because the meaning must be made one's own. Deliverance is expressive because it provides a context for the creation of meanings, but it is also reflective because that context is a cultural time perspective. When Kazantzakis states that absolute freedom is insupportable, he echoes the existentialist preoccupation with responsibility and its burdens. When he asserts that the human being must be determined in order to be of some "use," he echoes the utilitarian concern for achievement and results. When made the bases of philosophies of life, freedom and deliverance become respectively authentic existence (the Cretan glance) and the "will to believe" (submitting to the cry of the times). Authentic existence is, for Kazantzakis, associated with the flesh. Living in freedom involves contraction to the specious present in which the "individual" is asserted as a power of transcendence. The will to believe is joined to the spirit. Living for deliverance involves expansion into the past-present-future, the sacrifice of the present "individual" to the "person." Paradoxically, freedom and deliverance reverse the signs of ownness and the hunger for immortality. Contraction to the specious present emphasizes the infinite process of self propulsion, limited by nothing but its failure to be determined by an end. Expansion into the past-present-future allows for the expression of a particular table of values.

The paradox that when considered practically ownness is

transformed into freedom and the hunger for immortality into deliverance can be explained by the contradictory nature of these two ideals. Expression has nothing of its "own" but reflection. Hence, when deprived of any particular content all that can be expressed is the process of reflection, the freedom to transcend. Similarly, only when some meaning is projected does expression have a context in which to name and discriminate the flow of experience. When cultural time perspectives collapse, transpersonal meaning becomes a function of the will to believe. Yet the will to believe is checked by freedom, which makes that will always provisional. The rebellious self, the *expression of reflection*, continually asserts itself, in the terms of Dostoevsky's underground man, to "destroy" the systems of meaning that might have offered deliverance. Contrariwise, the "person," the *reflection of expression,* bears new visions forward, reigniting the will to believe. While the "flesh" or the "individual" declares each system to be a "gumdrop," the "spirit" or the "person" responds by regarding it as a "higher rhythm." Liberation from the continual *zozobra* between freedom and deliverance, the individual and the person, authentic existence and the will to believe, can be achieved only by submission to the truth of a single system of transpersonal meaning or by finding a substitute for cultural time perspectives. The first alternative is a dead option for those who have made the explosion of meaning their own. The second has yet to be fully explored.

Kazantzakis not only had an implicit ontology, which is shared by such disparate thinkers as Dostoevsky, Melville, and Kafka, but he also had a distinctive method of philosophizing. He attempted to make each system of transpersonal meaning his own by expressing it in his own words, transforming it into a personalized vision, and then following its discipline so as to experience the quality of life that it contained beneath its conceptual shell. In this sense he was faithful to his image of an Odysseus wandering from one place to the next, accumulating experiences but never put-

THE IMPLOSION OF MEANING (2)

ting down stakes and building a home. Rather than being an adventurer in space, he was an explorer in time, experiencing a series of cultural time perspectives but never allowing himself to heed the siren's song of deliverance. Each time that he might have gained repose, he rebelled as an underground man, divesting himself of his determinations, collapsing into the specious present, and asserting his freedom as a particular "man of flesh and bone." Kazantzakis used his method of personalizing meaning systems as a means of vaulting himself out of the suspended state of freedom and into another experiment in deliverance. He was so concerned with deliverance that he did not notice what had happened to him through each successive trial. As variegated and unstable as his life and thought were, he had a tough and immobile "conventional ego" that gave him strength, but also froze him into an immutable sameness or "identity." He lived by and for his torment, agony, and *zozobra*, which provided him with a form into and out of which each successive content could be poured. Along with Unamuno and Stirner, who also conceived of philosophy as spiritual autobiography, he inverted the quest for meaning, choosing a life of conflict and contradiction over one of faith in harmony and consistency. He was what might best be called an "agonist," deriving meaning out of the ambiguous and contradictory structure of his being rather than out of dedication to an ideal.

Agonism is as much a system of transpersonal meaning as those that it opposes and uses. Its distinctive stance towards the public situation is one of continual doubt and criticism. Its political consequence is the philosophical renegade who is nurtured by cultural time perspectives but then turns against them and destroys them by revealing them as mere hypotheses for individual experimentation and appropriation. The renegade is an anarchist who inverts images of the public situation by dissolving every group into its constituent individuals, leaving them free to recombine, if they will, on their own terms. Yet the agonistic renegade cannot live

102

but as a parasite on the very systems that have been deprived of their truth value. The agonist is a perpetual critic who must affirm the object of criticism. Agonists are masters of what Gregory Bateson calls the "double bind." With one hand they proffer criticism and with the other they offer inducements to deliverance. They affirm and deny simultaneously, rendering every project and effort at collective transcendence ambiguous while also declaring it to be necessary. They make myths of all systems, but refuse to mystify, console, and provide comfort. The agonist seeks universality by negating every particular determination, but, paradoxically, cannot make of the renegade's project a universal law of reason. The agonistic life seeks to liberate the concrete human being from the "conventional ego," but makes of torment and contradiction a new conventionalism. The agonistic life absorbs all meanings and perspectives into itself, but remains fundamentally changeless.

Although it has been embraced fully and explicitly by only a small number of philosophers, most of them figures associated with literature, agonism is the most complete response to the explosion of meaning. Its philosophy of history is essentially a commentary on the explosion of meaning and the attendant collapse of any outlet for what Santayana called "superhuman" interests, such as the desires for deliverance, immortality, recompense for suffering, and universal significance. These desires, all of which have been aggregated into the search for transpersonal meaning in the modern era, are products of the essential instability of human existence deriving from the polar opposition between expression and reflection. For agonism, history is the story of transpersonal meaning, a tale that continues as human beings come successively to understand that they must create their own time perspectives rather than insert themselves into preexistent contexts. Yet a cultural time perspective of one's own is a contradiction in terms. Transpersonal meaning is not something that can be created, but it must be encountered as something that is ordained. Hence, agonists

THE IMPLOSION OF MEANING (2)

appreciate various systems of meaning; they do not have *allegiance* to them. They maintain, however, a nostalgia for the community of meaning that has collapsed while they simultaneously do everything that they can to destroy the last vestiges of that community and to abort the emergence of any new one. For the agonist, the next chapter in history is the struggle to resist systems of transpersonal meaning and to strip people of their conventional egos or cultural *personae* so that they can confront one another directly as agonized and tormented "men of flesh and bone," contradictory composites of "individuality" and "personality."

The agonistic life, being indifferent to the content that is poured into and out of its form, is also indifferent to its own development as a temporal process. With each of his experiments in deliverance, Kazantzakis gained a new appreciation of existence; he changed qualitatively and became someone other than what he was. His obsession with deliverance seems to have blocked him from attending to the mutations of his own being, noticing the greater "breadth" of his existence, and turning his expanded appreciation of life to greater appreciation of the other people he encountered. He took from others the meanings that they could offer him in the hope of being able some day to give them what he considered to be the greatest gift of all: a universal meaning for life and death. Yet his agonistic approach to life precluded any possibility that the gift would ever be bestowed. He did not engage in the more modest task of helping other people to complete their own meanings by the experience that he could offer them. Perhaps his obsession with deliverance made him depreciate his experience since it did not provide him with the salvation that he refused to accept.

The method of personalizing perspectives and systems of transpersonal meaning that was used by such agonists as Unamuno, Stirner, and Kazantzakis for their ideal ends of satisfying the hunger for immortality, achieving "ownness," and gaining deliverance can be detached from these ends and made an end-in-itself, an intrinsic value. The agonists

104

were primarily concerned with the creation of a self to be projected into the past-present-future. While they were aware to the point of torment that perpetual creation, the permanent revolution of the self, involved as its logical implication destruction of the present self, they devoted all of their efforts to making permanent what they acknowledged to be transitory. Stirner pathetically characterized himself as a "creative nothing," but struggled to possess himself and embittered himself in the process. Unamuno and Kazantzakis both gazed into the "abyss," but strove to escape from it and "ascend" to the "summit of tragedy." Directed towards a contradictory self affirmation, either as preservation or perpetuation, they ignored their dependence upon others for the contents of their lives. Kazantzakis's project of making his life a gift to humanity, rather than to any particular human being, and his reluctance to acknowledge the gifts that others had bestowed upon him, is the extreme consequence of devoting one's life to transpersonal meaning when it is not possible for the human being to take any cultural time perspective for granted. Unamuno's "tragic sense of life," the polemical struggle between individual and person, blocked him from retaining any of the experiences that he had gained when ripping through and exhausting successive perspectives. Stirner made what possessed him "his own" only so that he could "get rid of it." Each one of the agonists viewed himself primarily as a creator, deriving justification from his uniqueness and ability to bear suffering and maintain independence.

The creative life is a hangover from the modern paradigm of a practical viewpoint directed towards realizing transpersonal meaning. It is ironic that for all of their obsession with creativity, the agonists and the more analytical formalists created very little. Their contribution has been, paradoxically, to destroy what had been created through the centuries preceding them and to expose the minimum structure of conscious experience: the dissolution and reconstruction of the subject-object polarity in successive "specious" presents. Yet if the agonists and formalists created little, they appreciated much. In their desperate efforts to reclaim transpersonal meaning, they revealed an alternative life philosophy that they could not bring to expression: existence as appreciation.

Relativization

Adopting a cultural time perspective, even as an experiment, is not only a process of directing one's life towards a particular end and of separating what is significant to express from what is not, but it is also a process of experiencing certain sentiments, emotions, and dispositions rather than others. Each system of transpersonal meaning is a table of values and a description of the problems and dilemmas involved in striving to achieve these values. Orientation of action within a particular cultural time perspective generates a specific quality of life, a specific organization and determination of passions, volitions, and emotional tone. Philosophy has been traditionally concerned with the cognitive and moral dimensions of cultural time perspectives, seeking to judge them according to criteria of factual accuracy, logical consistency, and comprehensiveness, or according to their ethical principles. Aesthetic criticism has been confined primarily to "works of art" and has been a minor branch of philosophy almost completely neglected in human ontology and political theory. Stressing cognitive and moral criticism has the consequence of emphasizing the reflective aspect of the self process over the expressive, because the aim of determining truth and rectitude is to demonstrate how one must or should act or project oneself into the past-present-future.

Aesthetic clarification, on the other hand, refers mainly to present expression: it gives a reading of the varieties of joy and suffering, hope and fear, love and hatred. From the viewpoint of public action, in which human beings are classified into different social orders such as citizenship, class,

106

nationality, and functional group, aesthetic clarification is subordinate to questions of instrumental, legal, and moral rationality. However, from the viewpoint of the "flesh and bone" human being, nothing is more important than the directly experienced quality of life: the feelings of frustration or consummation, regret or satisfaction, resentment or solidarity, unity or dispersion, distrust or fidelity. Even with regard to such "boundary conditions" as death, human beings are often less perplexed about the "meaning" of their finitude than with how they will dispose themselves towards dying: whether they will feel terror or confidence, whether they will resist with anguish or resign themselves peacefully.

The aesthetic dimension of human existence exceeds any atomistic or uni-dimensional reductions of it, such as the Freudian pleasure principle, the utilitarian hedonic calculus, or the positivistic notion of emotional ejaculation. All such accounts of feeling are ways of reducing it to a means to action. Having isolated and segregated certain responses from what F.S.C. Northrop called "the aesthetic continuum," instrumental and pragmatic accounts of feeling can be turned into programs for containing and conditioning action. However, when they are successfully implemented, they impose their own organization of quality on individuated human existence, albeit a deprived quality to which the political engineers are indifferent.

Similarly, more idealistic theories of emotions simplify the appreciative life by subordinating it to abstract structures such as the logical compatibility or contradiction between motives, evaluations, or duties. Such frameworks as cognitive dissonance or congruity theory do not accord expression an independent life, but superadd such feelings as discomfort or happiness to logically contradictory or consistent judgments or projects. Not only do the idealistic theories fail to acknowledge the degree to which ambivalence and ambiguity permeate human beings, but they also regard feeling as a formless mass that is organized only by the abstract categories of logical reason or, at best, by the

THE IMPLOSION OF MEANING (2)

dialectical structure of Platonic interpersonal or Hegelian intergroup dialogue. While the idealistic theories do recognize that the appreciative life exceeds any particular system of organization, they regard the excess negatively as a "blooming and buzzing confusion," not as a surplus of expression over what the practical viewpoint allows to be reflected.

Only a few twentieth-century philosophers have acknowledged that the appreciative or aesthetic dimension of human existence has a structure at least partially independent of logical or instrumental reason. Such overlooked thinkers as Elijah Jordan, James K. Feibleman, and Jose Vasconcelos developed conceptions of an appreciative logic which they opposed to formal logic. Jordan contrasted "analogical identity" to logical identity, Feibleman opposed "connotative inference" to denotative inference, and Vasconcelos differentiated "organic logic" from conceptual logic. Each of these conceptions of an appreciative order presupposes that the primary process of human existence is what Vasconcelos called the process of coordinating heterogeneous elements, or what is here named expression. Appreciative logic cannot be defined with the precision of its formal counterpart, but only by allusion and illustration, because it is not itself a perspective, but the foundation of all perspectives.

Each system of transpersonal meaning organizes the aesthetic dimension of human existence by providing it with a theme that is individuated and varied by the human beings allied with it. Each variation on the theme is analogically identical to the others. For example, the theme of Marxism, from the viewpoint of the individuated human being, is the struggle to overcome alienation. Regardless of the truth value of Marx's analysis of crises in the capitalist economic system or the plausibility of the Marxist theory of class struggle, each human being can directly experience alienation, not as an abstract category, but as a determination of experience made uniquely individual by a particular past and present. Alienation can be appropriated by human beings as

THE IMPLOSION OF MEANING (2)

their "own" only if they can specify it in terms of a particular loss of control over their circumstances. However, exemplification of the concept in one's concrete life experience is only a necessary condition for assimilating it. The sufficient condition is that alienation be expressed by the human being as a focal point for orienting the entire aesthetic dimension. One must feel a sense of separation from a desired unity, one must suffer the loss of control, one must be impelled to heal the divisions, one must be consumed by the will to solidarity, one must "see" the evidence of alienation everywhere and come to the realization that one is frustrated from the realization of potentials.

Revolutionary organizers may find it expedient not to attend to the aesthetic transformations wrought by revolutionary theory, because they are concerned only with mobilizing for action. However, "class consciousness" is, or might be, deeper than the superficial decision to ally oneself with a movement because it represents reason in history or promises material improvements or even presents a stirring moral ideal or meaning. Class consciousness, when interpreted as an aesthetic determination, is consciousness of the concrete way in which class relations have penetrated one's inner experience. It is awareness of the ways in which other human beings have entered one's life and structured one's experience relative to their projects. Appreciating class analysis is not making it one's own in order to get rid of it or to pass it over as one more "gumdrop," but to suffer individually the consequences that it notes and then to strive to surmount those consequences.

Appreciating a perspective does not mean making a "myth" of it in the sense that Sorel used the term. The appreciative life works in opposition to the mystified life. As Sorel describes myth in his *Reflections on Violence*, it is a unitary experience that takes over human beings and sweeps them along into a current of collective action. Each one becomes a homogeneous particle in an active mass. Appreciation of perspectives adds complexity to each existence and individuates it further by revealing new modes of relatedness and accompanying volitions and sentiments. It falls away from the "practical viewpoint" not by releasing reflective controls, but by directing reflection away from immediate action and towards clarification of the present. Appreciation also does not romanticize or "poetize" perspectives. It reveals what William James called their "cash value" in the coin of experience.

The dynamics of appreciation that were illustrated by the example of Marxist class analysis hold equally for every other cultural time perspective and system of transpersonal meaning. The neopositivistic model of structurally and functionally differentiated society can be incorporated by the individual as the theme of role conflict, self division, and pluralization of experience, while the conservative model of mass society can be appropriated as the theme of anomie. Such concepts as alienation, role conflict, and anomie were developed by their creators as accompaniments to general theories of social structure, as the subjective reflections of institutional dynamics. From the individuated human being's viewpoint, however, they are not accompaniments but the lived experiences that determine their existence. Anomie, for example, is not merely an inference about subjective "states" that cannot be "observed," but a condition that is suffered and agonized over by particular people. It is not a "postulated entity" like some subatomic particles are, but what Max Scheler called a "unit experience": an organization of the quality of individual life. It is not a "variable" that "explains phenomena" such as suicide, but what William James called an experience *fringing* and melting into suicide. Normlessness is a condition of human life that can lead to life's annulment.

Appreciation of perspectives is a process of "relativization," of holding systems of transpersonal meaning relative to oneself as a concrete durational being with a unique history and particular circumstances and determinations. Each perspective gives names to unit experiences that may have

characterized moments of a life and then organizes sentiments, volitions, and descriptions of interhuman relations
around the experiential center. Appreciation involves trans-
valuating as much of one's life experience as possible in
terms of the perspective, of creating a spiritual autobiography out of the problems and struggles that it identifies. At the
limiting point where it is no longer possible to make the
perspective one's own, one must call upon imagination to
stretch the boundaries of experience by devising analogies
between what has been assimilated and what has not yet
been "melted down" and expressed. The appreciative imagination extends the aesthetic dimension beyond the individuated human being to the other person.

Appreciation is not directed towards action or towards
finding a meaning to structure existence, but towards bringing past events and future possibilities into expression in the
expanded present of experience rather than the "specious"
present of action. It is a process of remembrance and fantasy disciplined by the concrete determinations of one's life
defined by particular patterns of relations: primary group
relations for psychiatric relativization, secondary group relations for sociological relativization, and historical relations for
cultural relativization. Appreciation of perspectives is an
inclusive rather than an exclusive process. Each relativization that is undertaken creates a uniquely determined, free-
standing, and absolute spiritual autobiography or, as Sartre
calls it, a "totalization" of experience. Successive relativiza-
tions express multiple autobiographies, each one of which is
logically exclusive of the others and practically incompatible
with them. Yet they are *aesthetically compatible* and even
mutually reinforcing, each one bringing to clarity new unit
experiences, organizing hitherto disparate contents, and
intensifying and expanding the "breadth," "ambiguity," and
"depth" of consciousness.

While creation requires possibilities to be narrowed, appreciation requires that they be widened and concreted into
lived duration. Bergson's notion that logically contradictory
motives and definitions are fused in the "fundamental self" is

THE IMPLOSION OF MEANING (2)

verified in the conscious process of appreciation and relativization which does not "invert" the practical viewpoint and split it into its component processes, but reverses it away from overt action in a public situation and towards the clarification of the implosion of that situation into the human being. Appreciation is a process of making meanings constituents of one's durational being by melting them down into sentiments and volitions: expressing them and coordinating them into felt wholes by analogy and connotative "fringes."

The self definition that results from relativization of perspectives is too complex and heterogeneous to form a stable identity for projection and propulsion into the past-present-future. Each unit experience that can form the focus of a life is counterbalanced by several others that limit it. Experience takes on the character of William James's "pluralistic universe" in which varieties of sentiments, volitions, and ideas fuse together to form systems, but exclude other complexes: experience is neither congeries of elements related externally by association, nor a coherent system deduced from immutable axioms. The most general categories that can be used to describe the appreciative self are "breadth" and "ambiguity." Breadth, a term that Dostoevsky uses throughout his novels to describe characters that incorporate contradictory motives ranging from individual self assertion to mystical communion and self sacrifice, connotes the qualitative diversity that marks a concrete and unique life submitted to appreciative clarification of its multiple relations. Ambiguity, the central category in Melville's novels, refers to the multiple and often opposing meanings that can be attached to any particular event, appearance, or symbol. Appreciation devolves the practical viewpoint into greater complexity by increasing awareness of the experiences that might be brought forward and projected into the past-present-future. As such, it is a counterweight to those tendencies in human existence that consolidate the self into a discrete and sharply defined actor performing specific functions within a fixed social structure and system of transpersonal meaning.

Relativization is not a process of reducing human beings

to social, psychological, or cultural "types," but rather a way of absorbing all such typifications into the flow of experience. Typifications are used politically and ideologically as "attributions" intended to function as controls on behavior and even on sentiment, as when a human being adopts a self image that has been fabricated by an organization, such as the "new socialist man" or the "company man." Resistance to typification has normally taken the form of the "underground man's" rebellion aimed at asserting self will, ownness, or superhuman interests, such as Unamuno's hunger for immortality. Appreciative resistance to typification and reduction does not involve a strategy of isolation, but one of incorporation. The richer and more complex the appreciative life becomes through the process of clarifying multiple relations to the public situation, the less the human being can be typified and exhausted by any one perspective.

Relativization can be distinguished from such formalist attempts to confront the explosion of meaning as Mannheim's "relationist" epistemology. Mannheim attempted to create a "perspective of perspectives" or metaperspective by correlating adherence to different meaning systems with social position. His approach was almost completely spatialized and involved such images as rising above partisanship and the "free-floating" intellectual. He hoped to combine partial systems into a dynamic totalization that would change with the appearance of new interests and social structures that represented them. The "Mannheim problem," which refers to the contradiction of claiming that all perspectives are relative to social position and that there is also a perspective free from relativity, is a result of the spatialized imagery of position. If cognition is made relative to *circumstance* (what surrounds the person) or situation (the person's site or position), there is no possibility of removing oneself from a particular location. Relativization, however, is not a spatialized process, but a temporal one that expresses the unit experiences attached to each perspective in an expanded present that grows richer with each new incorporation. Relativization never achieves absolute knowledge, because it is limited by the degree of complexity and diversity of past and present relations and by the barriers to imagination posed by social control mechanisms such as force, structured inequality, terror, and ideological monopoly. Insofar as a human being is able to connect the unit experiences defined by cultural time perspectives with some remembered or present experiences, relativization of those perspectives is possible, although imagination may be necessary for fuller appreciation. In cases of perspectives that define unconscious processes, appreciation involves not only concretization and expression of concepts, but also self criticism.

Appreciation may be considered as a process of "representing" other lives as well as one's own in present conscious experience. It is the process that allows human beings to transcend their pasts, not by creating a contribution or a gift, but by assimilating and expressing the consequences of their actual or possible relations. It is, in fact, the presupposition of creativity, because in order to form a project and execute it, it is necessary first to have expressed it and at least to some degree to have made it one's own by experiencing its quality. As Bergson pointed out, the human being is always a qualitatively distinctive and unique durational being simply by virtue of having organized quality in time. Appreciation does not destroy that uniqueness, but makes it richer and more complex, first by bringing neglected or repressed experiences into awareness and second by expanding the range of experiences by the use of analogical imagination through which similarity "melts into" individuality.

The Concrete Durational Being

The idea of a human being that results from the previous discussion of expression and reflection, and creation and appreciation, is that of a *concrete durational being* bringing experience to expression in a present and then projecting it

114

into a past-present-future. Human existence is an unstable compound of disparate and opposing processes that are synthesized temporarily into the "practical viewpoint" but that fall apart from one another on close examination. What we call a human life is the perpetual struggle and reconciliation of expression and reflection, the centripetal and centrifugal dynamics of experience and action through which meanings are organized and dissolved. This dialectic of mutual antagonism and mutual complementarity is the core of our being, bordered by the inhuman and the antihuman, both of which also compose us and complicate our instability. The concrete durational being is a unique and mutating compound or composite of what has been expressed and reflected in action and what has been melted down into appreciation by the analogical imagination, as well as what has been conventionalized into psychological, social, and cultural types. The more conventionalized the human being is made, the less the human being appears in self awareness and the awareness of others as a unique configuration of quality. Yet (and here Stirner was correct), each individual is a "unique one" simply by virtue of having coordinated quality in time. The breadth, depth, and ambiguity of appreciation varies according to the freedom and discipline of the analogical imagination, but the uniqueness of lived quality is a constant uniting all concrete durational beings. The "notes" or characteristics of a concrete durational being are lust (the inhuman), expression, reflection, and idealization (the antihuman). Reinterpreting the terms of R.G. Collingwood, the descent to lust is savagery, the flight to idealization is barbarism, and the sustenance of the expressive-reflective dialectic is civilization.

Lust, which has appeared as a category in twentieth-century thought under such names as the Freudian "id" or Santayana's "primal will," does not refer here only to sexual energy, but to those incomprehensible dynamics within our being that defy organization into complexes of quality, that cannot be brought to expression, but can simply be suffered.

THE IMPLOSION OF MEANING (2)

In the intuition that severs expression from reflection, lust appears as a blind, deaf, and dumb (senseless) force of dispersion that threatens to overwhelm and swamp expression, dissolving it and carrying it into a void, or what such writers as Dostoevsky, Tolstoi, and Melville, who appeared to have experienced it, called a "black hole." Freud, whose images of Eros and Thanatos oppose what are here called appreciation and lust, gave better expression to the inhuman dynamic of human being than any other twentieth-century thinker, and perhaps overemphasized it. Yet his analysis, though one-sided and often mechanistic, can be ignored only at the peril of deliverance to terror. Modern relativistic systems of transpersonal meaning, such as Marxism and positivism, which associate lust with sociocultural imperfections, encounter its facticity when they are made operative principles of regimes.

Lust consumes its object, rather than expressing it, and the ultimate object for lust to consume is human being itself. Its dynamic is controlled spontaneously by the inclusive, coordinative, and image-making process of expression, and deliberately by the manipulative and sanctioning process of reflection, particularly when it becomes conventionalized into mechanisms of social control. At the boundaries of conscious experience, lust is controlled by reflection through directing it towards the insatiable appetites for such abstract and extrinsic values as money, power, influence, and loyalty, and by expression through the hunger for immediate sensual gratification. It may be sublimated by ascetic disciplines that spiritualize it as the "void" or projected as the will to nihilistic destruction, but it remains in conscious life as the mark of expression's failure. The negativity of lust is not adequately comprehended in the idea of "nothingness" or in the notion of logical negation. The black hole into which Tolstoi's Ivan Illych saw himself being swallowed is as direct an experience as any other, if not more so, although, paradoxically, it cannot be described.

Lust is the pretemporal or atemporal. It draws human

116

being out of space and time; it is a self-consuming process that can only be imperfectly expressed in the present and projected into the past-present-future. Every failure to express, to appreciate, to represent meaning, and to accord attention is a sign of lust. From a mythical viewpoint lust is that which makes reflection both possible and necessary. The "conventional ego" creates space to maintain a discrete individual against the onslaught of lust.

While lust is the inhuman aspect of human being, idealization is its antihuman dimension. Idealization refers to what Bergson called "homogeneous" space and time, the abstraction of form from the context of past-present-future created by reflection to compose the practical viewpoint. Idealization becomes independent of appreciation in such mathematical systems as non-Euclidean geometries, which cannot be expressed and "melted down" into the flow of experience, but only *symbolized*. Such systems only enter experience indirectly through physical science and the technologies that can be invented by applying its experimental results. The closest approximation to idealization in social life is the deliberate attempt to control human behavior on the basis of plans grounded in statistical indices and enforced by external rewards and punishments (behavioral and social engineering). Such programs do not transcend the practical viewpoint, because they are grounded in conventional Euclidean space, but they represent what Gabriel Marcel called the "spirit of abstraction," the attempt to treat human beings as though they were merely behavioral organisms whose activity could be predicted and controlled in the same way as physical objects. Behavioral engineering, in its extreme form, neglects the durational being altogether, making contact with the individual only through the manipulation of inhuman lust (greed for abstract and extrinsic values, and craving for immediate sensual gratification).

The image of a "technocracy," a totalitarian regime based solely on behavioral engineering, is the contemporary substitute for the cultural time perspectives that have collapsed.

THE IMPLOSION OF MEANING (2)

The technocracy is *antitemporal*, playing upon and exploiting lust by reducing time to spatialized plans in which success is measured by the accumulation of means and by confining the individuated human being to a specious present. Technocracy is the limiting point of contemporary barbarism. It does not exist and will not unless spontaneous duration and expression are snuffed out. Technocracy is "unprincipled" in the sense that it has no end but the accumulation of means. In the contemporary era it is an ever-increasing component of political life, being joined to a multitude of regimes, each one representing and manipulating cultural time perspectives inherited from modern relativisms or traditional religions and using technocratic devices to achieve greater efficiency. As such regimes become pure attempts to project themselves in spatialized time (to maintain themselves), they will approach the technocratic limit and increasingly neglect the concrete durational being in favor of such negative ends as the mere survival of "humanity" in the abstract. Already the politics of fear and crisis and the idea that peace can be assured negatively by the threat of nuclear holocaust reveal that an obsession with death and lust rule the public situation.

The images of "energy crisis," "pollution," and "cancer" may be interpreted as merely external manifestations of a preoccupation with self destruction. Increasingly the world is haunted not by the specter of revolution, but by the specter of death itself as politics becomes backward-looking and retrospective, feeding upon regret that the earthly paradise promised by the idea of progress has slipped away, resentment that one's wishes are passed over in the juggling among organized interest groups, and revenge against inconvenient demands by insurgent groups that are simply the resultants of mass exploitative organization. The expansion of appreciation is blocked by the will to defend and maintain established privileges and the attendant project of repressing diversity through organized controls and formalistic procedures of "social accounting." The motto of the times is

THE IMPLOSION OF MEANING (2)

"backlash," the parasitical, regretful, and resentful reaction to change, the negation of Nietzsche's will to power and call to exert the effort to affirm the diversity, complexity, tensions, and agonies of the present. Death flourishes in the empty space of idealization, which is filled with containers such as concentration camps, prisons, and mental hospitals in which human beings are forced to contract their durational being to the minimum flash of self awareness.

The triumph of Pascal's spirit of logic over the spirit of finesse has not been complete, but the balance is turned increasingly in its favor through the imposition of modular time perspectives in which human beings are reduced to types that can be exhausted by *a priori* descriptions. Typification is inseparable from concrete durational being because it is the means by which reflection propels life into the past-present-future. However, when typification is used socially to restrict appreciation and to provide the last word on individuated human beings, it becomes an engine of repression at the service of death. Restriction of one's appreciation of others is a way of neglecting them by refusing to make them one's own. Restriction of the scope of others' appreciation of themselves, through attribution enforced by social controls, is a way of reducing them to objects for experiment and control. Restriction of others' appreciation of oneself is a strategy of isolation and fear. Restriction of one's appreciation of oneself is to make oneself an other to oneself. Each of these restrictions is a way of dying. Each is an integral aspect of human existence, because one direction of human being is irrevocably towards death. The practical viewpoint narrows and restricts: it is the realm of decision or what Justus Buchler called the "spoliation of the possible." In the contemporary era, however, the mask of death threatens to become the only *persona*.

Josiah Royce identified the "world of description" (physical reality) as the field of "materials of industrial art": substances postulated as enduring through time and sufficiently plastic to be modified and manipulated. He opposed to it the "world of appreciation" (social reality), which he defined as the realm of "sensitive appreciators of life." He remarked, looking back over the nineteenth century, that civilization had developed in such a way that the worlds of description and appreciation had become increasingly differentiated from one another. Human beings, he thought, had increasingly depersonalized nature and personalized one another. Writing at the same time, Alejandro Korn similarly observed that the nineteenth century had been characterized simultaneously by the reduction of thought to scientific rationality and the enhancement of human rights. Today the bifurcations identified by such sensitive observers as Royce and Korn are being resolved in favor of the reduction of human beings to materials of industrial art. Contemporary civilization, obsessed by the collapse of transpersonal meaning and consequently by death, suffers a radical failure of appreciation.

The failure of appreciation is a denial of and an attack upon concrete durational being, both as expressed in oneself and in the other. The struggles of such thinkers as Kazantzakis to "bring forth" a new meaning for life and death and thereby to set things right again are mirrored by a public situation in which totalitarian regimentation is either a persistent threat or a terrible actuality. The phenomenon of the "displaced person" and the "refugee" are represented philosophically by doctrines of "absurdity" and "absolute freedom," while the phenomena of the "concentration camp" and the "mental hospital" are represented by the abstract philosophies of science that are intended to provide a "reconstructed logic": a reformed, purified, and idealized order. Positivistic and analytical philosophies are as exclusionary with regard to the object of inquiry as conglomerate organizations are exclusionary with regard to the political object: the concrete durational being. The explosion of meaning has been encountered and managed by inattention and what Royce called "viciously acquired naivete" rather than by sensitive appreciation of life.

The great paradox of the twentieth century is the reverse

of that of the nineteenth. Socially and politically, ours has been a century of regimentation in which the paradigms of nineteenth-century positivism have been concreted into mass organizations and what "liberation" has occurred has been of, by, and for groups cemented by vanguards. Philosophically, however, the only new developments have turned on greater acknowledgment of freedom, responsibility, creativity, uniqueness, and personality, even if they have been truncated by concern about the problem of transpersonal meaning and have devolved the human being into the specious present. Totalitarianism, technocracy, and varieties of fascism and neo-fascism appealing to regret, resentment, and revenge have been the political novelties of our era. Tendencies towards acknowledgment of the concrete durational being have been the intellectual and aesthetic innovations expressed by such schools as surrealism, existentialism, phenomenology, process philosophy, and the less mechanistic variants of psychoanalysis. The examination of what Ortega called intrasubjectivity by such novelists as Unamuno, Kafka, Joyce, Faulkner, and Proust have expanded the opportunity for sensitive appreciation of life by revealing each author's unique durational being. The great twentieth-century novelists and their predecessors such as Dostoevsky and Melville do not offer transpersonal meanings or philosophies of history, but descriptions of their particular perplexities projected and diversified into characters and situations. One does not respond to their work by typifying it, but by appreciating them and, therefore, oneself. The way in which one can appreciate such novelists through assimilating their expressions is no different from the way in which it is possible to appreciate a concrete durational being, with the only exception that the other human being is a mutating world previous to one's own expression.

The Ambiguity of the Other

What might be called the "mysticism of life," as distinguished from the mysticism of the void and of death, captured the imagination of such writers as Dostoevsky, Unamuno, and Kazantzakis, all of whom glimpsed a vision of aesthetic perfection in which no content of experience would not be expressed and appreciated, in which there would be no disjunction between experience and action, and in which the practical and intuitive viewpoints would be merged. While this vision, which also inspired Bergson's later work, is the ideal that regulates appreciation, it is not a norm and cannot be made the principle of social life or even of individuated human existence. To attempt to idealize appreciation is to make of it a meaning to which concrete durational beings would be sacrificed. In the individuated human existence that we share with one another and sometimes sustain, we are always ambiguous towards ourselves and towards others. We struggle within ourselves to subdue lust long enough to create a tension between expression and reflection and then to fend off being typified and reduced to "materials of industrial art." Our relations with ourselves are social and mirror our relations with others. The same dialectic of mutual complementarity and mutual antagonism that marks the self process also characterizes the social process: the state is the individual writ large and the individual is the state writ small. The other is a source of expressions to be appreciated, but also a source of threats to be controlled. The other is a potential or actual appreciator, lending attention to our expressions, but also a possible tool to be exploited and manipulated from the practical viewpoint. We encounter our own self-consuming drive towards death as consumption of the other and the other's lust as negation of ourselves. We deploy the other on our social chess board and find ourselves to be pawns in other games. The more that appreciation is enhanced the greater is the "breadth" of experience that must be coordinated and the lesser is the proportion of experience that can be carried over into action.

The "vital self contradictions," as Santayana called them, of the appreciative life give it an uncertain and ambiguous quality that may be contrasted with the apparently unilateral lives of those who are oriented towards transpersonal mean-

122

ing and the barbaric lives of those who are directed towards the accumulation of extrinsic values. A meaningful life is led under the canopy of a cultural time perspective which makes specific the tensions within divided human beings and structures the individual's perplexities according to their relations with the table of values to be achieved. Kierkegaard's anguish, for example, was meaningful Christian anguish, structured in terms of his justification before God. Cultural time perspectives, then, do not eliminate agony, but organize it and endow it with meaning. For all of his vacillations, even Unamuno acknowledged the Christian perspective by rebelling against it and transmuting it into a vehicle for self expression. Similarly, Sartre has maintained a paradoxical relation with Marxism, transmuting the dictum that the freedom of each is the condition of the freedom of all into the declaration that none will be free until all are free and, hence, justifying his ambiguous attachment to that perspective. A barbaric life is led under the signs of the dollar, the gun, the insignia, and the slogan. It, too, structures agony by organizing it as a "war of all against all," projecting it outwards as a ceaseless search to establish the self in a mutually exploitative network. Only the appreciative life is multilateral, acknowledging countervailing processes and ambiguities in each human event.

Appreciation of the other involves the same methods as appreciation of oneself. The other must be encountered first through as many typifications as possible: social, psychiatric, and cultural. Appreciation of others, then, cannot be exhausted by clarifying one's orientation to them as actors relative to one's projects or even by appropriating their self images or self concepts. The self concept or "conventional ego" is an artifact of the practical viewpoint and represents only that organized content which the other projects into the public situation. Behind the self concept is the history of a concrete durational being who may not be aware either of that history or of the different perspectives that might illuminate it as alternative autobiographies. Frequently, if not al-

THE IMPLOSION OF MEANING (2)

ways, it is possible to appreciate others more than they appreciate themselves by attending to their expressions and judgments, and then placing these utterances into a variety of contexts. The other may be typed by multiple sociologies, psychiatries, and anthropologies, each of which provides hypotheses about the quality of the other's experience. None of these typifications and the inferences about experience that follow from them can exhaust the other or stand as definitive interpretations, but they are possible entry points into the other's concrete durational being. They indicate what the other's sentiments and volitions *might be*, not what they *are*. They also indicate qualities that the other may not be able to express now but might be able to express in the future.

Although it is not possible to initiate appreciation of others except by typifying them and then using the categories to penetrate to unit experiences, contextual interpretation is not sufficient. A concrete durational being cannot be exhausted by making a person into a "case," for example, of anomie, alienation, or role conflict, even when these terms stand for particular variations of the overall themes. The concrete durational being is not merely an exemplification of unit experiences, but a unique and continuously mutating being responsive to a multitude of relations that are brought into varying degrees of expression. The aim of appreciation is to risk a venture beyond possibilities and hypotheses to assimilate how the other has coordinated or failed to coordinate heterogeneous experience and what the other has been able to express. Appreciation of others requires that one attend to their utterances and deeds, not in order to predict what they will do in future situations and to formulate expectations about their behavior from a practical viewpoint, but in order to discern their surplus of expression over reflection: the possibilities that they have failed to realize, the other voices that are suppressed within them, the secret yearnings and regrets that they are afraid to reveal, and the accommodation that they have made between the mutually antagonistic

124

and complementary aspects of their experience. Such assimilation of others, making them one's own, is always imperfect and proceeds by listening and looking for clues to what is not disclosed, asking questions, watching for what might have been accomplished but was left undone, registering repetitive themes and then imagining that their opposites represent the others' deeper longings, and seizing upon paradoxical and contradictory utterances to identify experiences that have not yet been coordinated. Sensitive appreciation of another life demands attention to all of those utterances that the practical viewpoint condemns because they breed insecurity: equivocations, ambiguities, prevarications, lies, tautologies, begged questions, and oxymorons. All that cannot be defined and systematized points to the "loose ends" of experience that mark the failure of typification, the possibility for novelty, and the incompletion of expression.

Appreciation of the other reveals what has not yet been finished and what has not been and, perhaps, cannot be objectified and projected into the past-present-future. This revelation offers a basis for relating to others and to oneself that contrasts with the instrumental and exchange relations of organized public life. Whenever another person reveals "loose ends" there is an opportunity to grasp them and to cooperate with the person in bringing them into the fabric of expression. The failure of expression is also an invitation to participate in the construction of another life. Moreover, another person's equivocations may also be made one's own, opening up new dimensions of self criticism and compounding one's own "breadth" and "ambiguity." Typifications provide the contexts in which the specific insufficiencies of each concrete durational being unravel, but only attention to, acknowledgment of, and even acceptance of these insufficiencies as they are disclosed by "impractical" utterances constitute an appreciative life.

The appreciative life is drastically limited by the countertendency to establish oneself as a discrete actor projected into the past-present-future, to have one's demands met predictably and not merely appreciated, and to hold the other relative to one's own plans. The alternative to appreciating others is disposing of them, getting rid of them, tolerating their presence, respecting their rights, using them, and defining them for one's own purposes or for the realization of some impersonal idea. The highest point to which the ethic of meaningful life rises is the idealized imperative to treat others as ends-in-themselves, never as means only. In the absence of appreciation the Kantian principle means keeping up the social compact by resisting the temptations to lie, to steal, and to break promises (strict imperatives), and to kill or harm (meritorious imperatives). The moral life is from this viewpoint a strenuous refusal which is grounded in duty, sacrifice, and "practical reason," to place one's own advantage above that of others. One cherishes and fetishizes one's "good will" as an indestructible possession that is immune from the mutations of concrete duration. Yet the Kantian ethic is basically a defensive strategy or what Nietzsche called a "herd morality." It defines the self as a relation to conventions, such as property relations and contracts, and offers a nonviolent substitute for Hobbes's sovereign. From the pinnacle of the categorical imperative all other ethical systems based on meaning appear defective because they represent truces in the campaign of each one to reduce the others to instruments. The Kantian morality at least acknowledges human beings as ends-in-themselves, although it does so negatively by defining them as beings who might be capable of resisting the temptation to place themselves over and against others. The Kantian ethic of ultimate ends does not acknowledge concrete durational being and leaves the individual vacillating between lust and idealization; it is an eternal and universal law.

Although there is an appreciative life, there is no ethic of appreciation that can organize the practical viewpoint. The direction of the appreciative process is to express as much experience as possible. This implies that appreciation is fullest when not only one's own but the other's life is as broad

126

and ambiguous as it can be. It might appear that the imperative of appreciation would be: Act so as to bring to expression and into deed a plenitude of experience. However, the concrete durational being is a compound of lust, expression, reflection, and idealization. The concrete durational being can only will the mysticism of life in the optative mood: May it not happen that I neglect the other voices that might be raised within me. Yet these voices are continually being muffled in the process of projecting a *persona* into the past-present-future. Relations with the other are riddled with decision points at which one must acknowledge the limits of appreciation in lust and the resultant will to withdraw attention and erect systems of regulations backed by sanctions. One is also continually brought to realize that the other resists penetration out of fear of being used and consumed. Often the other "classifies" the most cherished expressions as secrets providing the untainted last resort for individuality. Appreciation negates itself and becomes a form of terror when it is made a duty or a crusade to "probe" the other or "pry" the other open. The appreciative life is a gift that can be cultivated by sharpening one's attention, but it is not a duty that can be willed or a "project" to which one can be loyal or faithful. The act of grasping the loose ends of another person's experience and then collaborating in weaving them together cannot be imposed upon the other, but must be freely accepted. There can be no imperative to enter where one is not welcome. Kantians can discharge their duties regardless of the dispositions of others. In contrast, "sensitive appreciators of life" are dependent upon the willing collaboration of others.

Although there is no appreciative ethic, the process of appreciation has moral consequences. An appreciative life regards any neglect of concrete durational being and any deprivation of breadth and ambiguity as sacrifices to be resisted when possible and to be borne unwillingly otherwise. To appreciate those who restrict expression is not to tolerate them, much less to welcome their endeavors. Appreciation engenders a kind of universal pity that is awakened whenever one becomes aware of the suppressed possibilities in the other person and, simultaneously, a rage against all of those activities that unite to suppress expression and that might be alleviated, moderated, or reduced. The extent to which pity and rage are translated into political action against power structures is dependent upon an estimation of one's capability. The notion of capability does not refer to the physical possibilities for success but to one's dispositions to tolerate being used by others, to surrender one's distinctive projects temporarily or altogether, to overcome one's fears, and, most importantly, to heighten one's generosity. Liberality and generosity are virtues that direct one not only to appreciate but to bring suppressed expressions to the surface. They substitute for duty the careless joy that appears when one is suddenly moved to overcome an obstacle or barrier that separates oneself from others. Generosity can mean as little as overcoming a fear so that one can participate in an activity with another or as much as representing another person so fully that one's own projection into the past-present-future is spontaneously effaced. Appreciation is a preparation for generosity because it awakens sensitivity to voices other than one's own "conventional ego," but it does not imply or command generous deeds, which arise unbidden.

Generosity, or what the Mexican philosopher Antonio Caso called "existence as charity" (*existencia como caridad*), is the summit of concrete durational being, the point at which the other person is brought into one's own existence so completely that the tortured vacillation between ownness and authenticity is transcended. Contemporary totalitarianism conspires and aspires to eliminate generosity even as a possibility by substituting for it identification with a collective or radical dependence upon organized facilities and benefits. Generosity is not satisfied with a meaningful insertion into a cultural time perspective, but only by a participation in another life. It does not relate human beings to one another

128

in a system of functions projected into the future, but unites them in an expanded present in which their attention is directed towards one another and not towards the next moment of an indefinite sequence. One cannot live for generosity as a meaning or justification, but one can live more or less generously.

Generosity momentarily eliminates the ambiguity of the other by allowing one's appreciation to be immediately reflected in a deed. When generosity fades into other experiences the ambiguity is severely restored and all of the tensions of the concrete durational being are exposed once again. The longing for transcendence is again displaced to the optative mood, but it resides there as a reminder that the loss of transpersonal meaning does not signify the plunge into the abyss or the encounter with the absurd. The appreciative life and the generous deed might be reflected as the axiology of some future civilization that would measure itself by their standard, by its ability to cultivate them, but they do not exist for this end. They exist because we are concrete durational beings who, among many other things, express one another to ourselves.

IV.

The Explosion of Meaning (2)

Why have I, a political philosopher by profession and vocation, found it necessary to turn my attention away from the public situation and back upon the processes that constitute human life or what I have called the concrete durational being? Political philosophy has traditionally been derived from the practical viewpoint and has addressed the problems of how a common life is possible and how it should be composed. The concepts upon which it has relied and which it has related in various ways, justice, the common good, rights, authority, and law, for example, have generally been absent from my preceding discussion. Their absence does not indicate purposeful neglect, but a judgment that the mark of the current public situation is a crisis of meaning.

The practical viewpoint, which has been the foundation for political studies (political philosophy was for Plato, Aristotle, Rousseau, Hegel, and Marx, among others, the study of how practice could be made rational, while for Machiavelli and Hobbes it was an inquiry into how practice is possible), is today in question. It has been analyzed by several generations of philosophers into its minimum structure: the perpetual reconstitution of subject and object, and their active synthesis in successive "specious" presents. The various types of formalism have revealed that human beings do not relate themselves to a preexisting meaning outside their activity, but that they create the common meanings to which they are committed by sanctions or to which they commit themselves voluntarily. The formalist critique has shown that

130

not only are people responsible for themselves, they are also responsible for one another. Yet it has provided no guidance as to how they can or should discharge this responsibility. Such guidance, which is the chief concern of any serious political philosophy, cannot be based upon a procedure of "methodical doubt," which tears down the practical viewpoint to its elemental structure and then reconstitutes it around some preceding cultural time perspective (Sartre's Marxism) or the quest for a new meaning (Kazantzakis's Odyssey). Political philosophers can accomplish their task only by a much more radical sort of doubt, what Unamuno called "agonic doubt," which questions stable and common meaning as the most important constituent of the public situation. Political philosophers, then, must assimilate and make their own viewpoints other than the practical, and then must attempt to relate these viewpoints to the public situation.

Political thinkers often forget that the twentieth century has been marked not only by an explosion of perspectives, but by an explosion of fundamental viewpoints. Past civilizations have experienced explosions of meaning, such as the clash between different philosophies of conduct in the Hellenistic era and in ancient China. However, previous ages of philosophical and cultural conflict were unified by common questions and starting points: the projects were the same, if not their contents. Stoics, Epicureans, cynics, skeptics, and neo-Platonists, for example, all proceeded by holding human existence relative to being and then interpreting how people should conduct themselves in accordance with how they related to being. Today the questions are relative as well as the answers. Phenomenologists and Marxists, for example, do not merely provide different responses to the same problems, but they begin from heterogeneous standpoints. They do not meet one another in debate on common ground, but reduce one another to their own terms and then perform a critique. There is no longer one philosophical community whose members may engage in dialogue or debate, but

THE EXPLOSION OF MEANING (2)

multiple philosophical "communes" relating to one another by mutual criticism. Current disputes in philosophy hinge upon mutually exclusive interpretations of what human beings *are*, not what they *do* or *should do*. Hence, political philosophers who avoid investigating ontology condemn themselves to being parasites on some unclarified theory of being.

The preceding chapters of the present study are attempts to show how meaning has come into question culturally and historically, how a self composing and projecting meanings is possible, and how other processes than meaningful action can direct a life, if not exhaust it. The search for a viewpoint to which practice could be held relative was resolved by an intuition that splits the practical standpoint into mutually antagonistic and complementary processes of expression and reflection. The present investigation has made human beings appear to be far more complex than have previous theories. The concrete durational being is, as Vasconcelos said, a process coordinating heterogeneous elements. But this simple definition conceals the multitude of paradoxes, tensions, and ambiguities that qualify the coordinative process and make its adequate description a goal worthy of Bergson's proposed intuitive science.

As Kant said Rousseau was the Newton of the moral world, one might equally claim that Bergson was the Planck or Heisenberg of human existence. Bergson was the first to perceive the need not only to critique the notion of the self rationalistically as Hume and later empiricists had done, but to intuit the processes constituting the self by abandoning the practical viewpoint. In his early work, he rigorously avoided the speculative reason of nineteenth-century system builders and the practical reason and logical reason of the twentieth-century thinkers who succeeded him and neglected his findings. Bergson, of course, did not grasp the implications of his own findings because he was so concerned with providing new answers for metaphysical questions. His promise to free the study of "life" from the analytical and experimental methods of the natural sciences was never fulfilled because he resorted to biological science rather than to intuitive phenomenology to elaborate his basic insight. His followers, such as Sorel, never took the trouble to recapture the intuition severing the "fundamental self" from the "conventional ego" and, therefore, distorted it by "spatializing it" in such concepts as "myth." Bergson's vitalism became a fad and, even worse, a legitimation for fascist movements. There is no purpose served by showing that Bergson's philosophy is contradictory to fascist glorification of the will, and that its opposition between two contrary self processes neutralizes political irrationalism. Even a superficial reading of his social philosophy, contained in *The Two Sources of Morality and Religion*, shows that the only kind of leadership that Bergson could consistently approve was the type of nonviolent appeal to charity and sacrifice represented in our century by such figures as Gandhi and Martin Luther King, Jr. Yet his thought was appropriated by fascists and was criticized by others on that basis, and this exploitation provides an example of how the necessarily impractical viewpoint of serious intuitive analysis can become a dangerous weapon when carried over unreflectively into the public situation.

The problem of political philosophy should be to find some way of bridging the intuitive and practical viewpoints so that the intrinsic value of expressive being will not be submerged by contrived systems of transpersonal meaning or, even worse, by the reduction of human beings to mere instruments in a social order composed by complex hierarchical organizations. This problem of mediating between intuition and practice has not even been addressed by the vast majority of social and political philosophers in the twentieth century because of their enslavement to nineteenth-century or earlier systems, or to formalism. The existential phenomenologists believed that they were making a revolution when they substituted being-in-the-world for the transcendental reduction, but they were merely restoring to prominence the

THE EXPLOSION OF MEANING (2)

"practical viewpoint" that Bergson had already acknowledged and criticized. Philosophers like Heidegger were
correct that the turn to what Santayana called the realms of
essence and spirit occurs within and is dependent upon
being-in-the-world. Santayana, who in many respects repli-
cated the work of existential phenomenologists through his
critique of transcendental idealism, thought of the contemplation of essences as an interlude in the life of a "psyche" or
mind-body constituted by a situation. Yet holding contemplation relative to being-in-the-world does not answer Bergson's claim that he discovered the processes constituting
being-in-the-world not by rising above them but by penetrating inside them. If Bergson is correct, his intuition is one that
while occurring within the practical viewpoint is not a mere
interlude disclosing possibilities but an insight into actual
constitutive processes. His intuition would then be more than
an extraordinary and intense experience. It would be an
insight into what makes our everyday life possible.

The difficulties involved in relating intuition to political
questions are the same that beset any effort to join the
impractical with the practical. While intuition is neither a
transcendental view of things *sub specie aeternati* nor a
mystical vision, it has in common with pure reflection and
mysticism a suspension of practice. Yet it is closer to the
practical viewpoint than the attitudes with which it might be
confused, because it is *intra-practical* rather than *extraprac-
tical*: it reveals the constituents of practice instead of a
supposed transcendence over it. The results of taking an
intuitive viewpoint are unequivocal for philosophical anthropology. Not only is the human being a practical animal with
the additional possibilities of disinterested contemplation and
ecstatic union, but a concrete durational being through
which disparate processes are dialectically related and of
which the practical viewpoint is always a simplification and
falsification. Not only is the human being one who has
unfulfilled possibilities, as the existentialists point out, but one
who has *unexpressed* possibilities. Not only is the human

134

being incapable of being reduced to an objective definition, but he or she is also incapable of being exhausted by a descriptive phenomenology. No psychoanalytic, sociological, or cultural perspective can give a complete account of a concrete durational being, who is the one who coordinates the experiences to which such perspectives obliquely refer. No descriptive phenomenology identifying modes of being-in-the-world can give a complete account of a being who constitutes practice. Yet while philosophical anthropology is enriched by intuition, political philosophy seems to be at least two removes from it, because politics is active reflection upon practice: the activity of determining what activities will be permitted into the public situation. As such, politics has no direct relation with any impractical viewpoint, whether transcendental, mystical, or intuitive.

The subject of philosophical anthropology, or as I would prefer to call it, "human ontology," should be the concrete durational being. The subject of political philosophy, however, cannot be the concrete durational being because politics only deals with individuals as social actors. Politics and, therefore, political philosophy cannot reach beyond what Bergson called the "conventional ego" and most frequently they do not even reach that far. Political philosophy has been and will inevitably remain a nest of abstract conceptions of human existence derived from or generative of legal fictions. This limitation on political philosophy, the dethronement of it as the "master science," is not to be deplored and lamented, but welcomed as an indication that politics wÍll never be able to speak to us about the most significant features of our being. Political relations, even the best instances of civic friendship and voluntary and cooperative participation, cannot determine, although they may encourage, appreciation and generosity. The first contribution of intuitive analysis to political philosophy is to limit severely its scope. Any pretensions by political philosophers to provide solutions to the agonies of human existence break against the interior tensions and uniqueness of the concrete durational being. Political philosophers have the choice of making room for experiences that their systems cannot even describe or to suppress these experiences through intellectual terror. Such intellectual terror goes hand-in-hand with the physical terror of totalitarian regimes and of the totalitarian islands or continents in other contemporary political orders.

Any possible bridges between the evidence of intuition and political philosophy cannot be constructed before the nature of the latter's object—politics—has been clarified. At present it is sufficient to note that the mediations will be those aspects of social life that qualify and restrict politics in its pure form. But what is pure politics?

Politics

Politics, I repeat, is active reflection upon practice: the activity of determining what activities will be permitted into the public situation. Political philosophy is inquiry into the principles that should and do guide that determination. Politics, then, is devoid of expression: it is reflection upon what is reflected into action by concrete durational beings. Another way of stating this definition is that politics is the *deliberate and effective allocation of values and vocations.* As with any definition of a human activity (each type of human activity "fringes" into others in concrete experience), this one has a built-in imprecision based on the various possible interpretations of the term *deliberate.* Any definition of politics must preserve the notion of conscious and purposive decision. Yet to make conscious and purposive decision the hallmark of politics is to restrict it too narrowly and to leave out cases in which the allocation of values and vocations is deliberately left to supposedly private determination. Even then the definition might be too narrow and it might be more accurate to include cases in which the allocation of values and vocations was ignored through processes of viciously acquired naiveté. As Josiah Royce noted, a close analysis of experi-

136

ence reveals many instances of deliberate forgetting. The diverse interpretations of the term *deliberate* point to the necessity of not allowing formal and obvious institutional decisions to restrict the scope of political investigation while also maintaining some boundary between politics and other activities such as work, inquiry, worship, recreation, and a host of others.

The idea that politics is the deliberate and effective allocation of values and vocations contrasts with David Easton's notion that politics is "the authoritative allocation of values." The terms *deliberate* and *effective* have been substituted for *authoritative* in order to expand politics to include all of those instances in which decisions are made and enforced (even by neglect) about what human beings will be permitted, compelled, or encouraged to do or have. The present discussion is not informed by a desire to provide a scope for political science as opposed to any other discipline. Politics is a process that can be organized and institutionalized in a multitude of ways and that appears in a large proportion of human relations. R.D. Laing, for example, has correctly and brilliantly identified political processes within intimate relations. Easton's idea that "parapolitical" processes should be distinguished from politics as such has the normative bias of emphasizing authority over power. Deliberate and effective allocation may be based on authority, power, expediency, or even routine compliance, none of which necessarily determine the acts of decision and enforcement. Of course, the notion of deliberate and effective allocation has the normative bias of remaining neutral between functionalism which stresses authority and conflict theory which stresses power. It is neither adapted to an apology for existing institutions nor to an attack upon them. In some situations, however, it might be a practical ground for questioning establishments, and in others it might be a basis for neutralizing commitment to change. No definition of politics is "value neutral" because politics is practical and uses definitions of politics as means of control and persua-

THE EXPLOSION OF MEANING (2)

sion. The present definition is not meant to supersede others but to indicate that dimension of the practical viewpoint least in contact with concrete durational being. Hence, it is dependent upon a human ontology, although it overlaps with definitions proceeding from different viewpoints, such as Arthur Bentley's notion that politics is "representative activity."

A second variation on Easton's idea is the addition of vocations to values. Following Harold Lasswell's lead, Easton defined politics as a distribution mechanism, but restricted what is allocated to goods. Unamuno saw the defect of such a narrow definition decades before Easton formulated it: "The deepest and gravest social problem, which is the basis of all of the others, is, perhaps, that of one's own vocation. The so-called social question is, perhaps, more a problem of the division of vocations than one of the division of wealth."[1] It should not be necessary to stress that politics not only determines who *gets* what, but who *does* what, and that Unamuno's emphasis on doing over having has become ever more plausible in an era of control by massive state, corporate, and educational conglomerates. Definitions of politics based on having are mystifications in liberal societies, but they are simply and obviously incorrect in contemporary administrative states.

When politics is divested of the principles of legitimacy provided by cultural time perspectives and systems of transpersonal meaning, its essence is revealed as control over *space* and the resources within it. *Politics is the process of deciding what will be allowed into space and what will be excluded from it.* Politics, then, is the least concrete human process, the one most subject to idealization, and the one that necessarily makes time a function of space. The legal fictions that precipitate from political processes are nontemporal entities that make contact with actual social relations only when control is exerted over other activities. Corresponding to abstract and specialized legal fictions that describe state institutions and their operations are the conventional attributions and stereotypes that human beings and

138

groups employ to keep one another in *place.* Politics exists in the spatialized time of five-year plans, ten-to-twenty-year sentences, and four-year terms. Political solutions are based on *where* people belong. The state is defined territorially, not durationally, although Hitler's "thousand-year Reich" demonstrated the consequences of taking spatialized time as the only time perspective. Lasswell's definition of politics as "who gets what, when, and how" is ironic in leaving out the spatial basis for all political decisions. Perhaps he assumed that the essential *where* would be understood. The spatial root of politics explains its association with force and coercion, the means of moving people from one space to another or eliminating them from space altogether. The term *coercion* is most directly derived from the Latin verb *coercere* (to surround).

Politics is not encountered as a dialogue or discussion about "what we should do together" or "what we should share in common," but as a determination of "what you will permit me or forbid me to do" or "what you will permit me or forbid me to have." What is called politics in everyday life often lacks the stark character of command and obedience because it is qualified by other human processes, but as long as there is at least one person who feels shut out of a situation or pushed into a corner, pure politics will be present. Ivan Karamazov's complaint against God and the underground man's attack on the crystal palace are the anarchist's charge against all who deny the root of politics in coercion. Yet coercion is not the only means of political control. People are kept in their places by the distribution of facilities in space, by limitations on the perspectives that they can assimilate, and by treating them as if they were merely examples of categories. Politics is always a denial of complexity and a determination of possible future relations. It is based on coercion, but it uses the model of coercion to deny in all aspects of human existence by analogous mechanisms such as censorship and procedures. The presence of political processes and their affirmation are the measure of tra-

139

gedy and failure in human existence. Yet this tragedy and this failure are willed by each against all and, hence, by all against themselves.

The preceding discussion of politics is intentionally radically Hobbesian. Its object, however, is not Hobbesian (to prove the rationality of a sovereign), but to abstract out of human affairs a process that is normally limited and qualified by other activities. Pure politics does indeed occur: it is not an analytical distinction. But its either/or character is most frequently attenuated, at least for those who are sufficiently privileged to have multiple projects and abundant desired alternatives to any activity from which they might be excluded. One's experience of pure politics is a function of one's options within a social structure. The more restricted is one's *mobility,* the more that one is subject to pure politics and is kept in place. Mobility, the ability to move and to occupy different positions in a social structure, is the objective definition of freedom in the contemporary world. Freedom to move into and out of social spaces, or to remain within them, is a function of one's resources to bring forward projects into actions.

The origin of politics from the individual's viewpoint is threat against or fear about someone's projection into the past-present-future. Hence, the individual wills control over space in order to maintain control over duration. For the individual human being, politics means that someone will be occupied in some way somewhere at a given point in spatialized time. The murderer who threatens duration itself will be in prison, the wife will be "in the kitchen," the black will be in "the ghetto" and outside one's "neighborhood," the Palestinians will be in their refugee camps, the Jews will be pushed "into the sea," the clients will "keep" their appointments. The political ideal, not the human ideal, would be to become Hobbe's sovereign who determines everyone's place but her or his own. All other human beings would be reduced to extensions and instruments of one's own projects and, therefore, would no longer be threats: the political ideal is effective and active solipsism. The others would be constants in the great experiment of one's own life.

The strictly political will may be unpleasant to acknowledge, especially in its extreme case. Sartre, for example, has been frequently ridiculed and scorned for identifying the primal human desire to be God. The political will is merely the secularization of Sartre's "useless passion" and represents reflection's demand for uninterrupted and infinite persistence or what Sartre called "transcendence." The will to be sovereign is limited by one's dependence upon others, but is only annulled by common participation in a system of transpersonal meaning and by appreciation of the other. Yet the history of our century has shown that active and effective solipsism can be exemplified in the "cult of personality" or the "leader principle." Some people have attempted to ignore their dependency and have failed to appreciate or to find any meaning beyond their own power.

Hobbes was correct in asserting that politics is based upon fear and manifested as the will to advantage and control. In psychiatric terms, politics is the central expression of the inferiority complex: one attempts to demonstrate and prove one's superiority in order to conceal one's anxieties from others and from oneself. Submission to political processes is grounded in fear and resignation, calculation of advantage, hopelessness, *ressentiment* (abstract duty concealing resentment), or the judgment that the political order is necessary to protect the flourishing of other human processes. The last ground for submission is the only rational foundation for politics and whether it is appropriate can only be known through appreciation of the other, which is always imperfect. Politics is indeed a "war of all against all" in which each one seeks to limit the other and is in turn limited by the other. Duty or abstract obligation means throwing a "veil of ignorance" over one's concrete durational being and treating oneself as an other. Obligation is proper for what Kant called a "rational being": an abstract being-in-space whose existence Kant himself doubted.

Politics is a war of all against all, but politics does not exhaust human existence. Its closest approach to other human processes is the abstract principle of obligation, which defines a formal solidarity that is based upon the practical viewpoint: each one is an "end" or a *pour soi* by virtue of projecting a meaning into the past-present-future. Political processes range between this formal idea and the mechanical aggregation of individuals held together by coercion or by dependence upon instruments (Sartre's "serial order"). In between are the more-or-less coercive "balances" of competing interests negotiated through the state structure. That many political theorists have believed that Kantian morality is politically utopian and that bargaining processes are the best possible means of achieving solidarity in the public situation is a symptom of the profound crisis of our age. Were the pluralists correct, the other person would indeed be "hell" and life would be "solitary, poor, nasty, brutish, and short." But human beings are not merely beings-in-space. They are concrete durational beings capable of acknowledging their relativity to others and not merely their abstract identity as so-called ends-in-themselves. Other forms of solidarity are based upon acknowledgment of relativity which, in the Bergsonian language, penetrate more or less deeply inside the concrete durational being.

Solidarity

By participating in social activities, human beings acknowledge practically their dependence upon others. Nobody is an active solipsist, not even a hermit who distinguishes between tools that were invented and made by others, and current sensory experiences; and between the tales that he or she recounts internally and various experiences upon which these tales are based. Those who live by their own rules and make their own products use symbols and tools to express and reflect themselves. Penetrating even more

142

deeply, the "conventional ego" is a precipitate of social relations that can be abolished only by eliminating the past-present-future. Yet acknowledgment of dependence and, therefore, of particularity and insufficiency does not mean acceptance of them. Political processes and relations are indications of a primitive impulse of individuals to separate themselves from others by absolutizing their processess of self transcendence or projection into the past-present-future.

The formal (abstract rights and duties) and mechanical (aggregation by coercion) solidarities formed by political relations are analogous to what Bergson called the method of "analysis and recomposition" in the process of inquiry. According to Bergson, natural scientists, as well as rationalist philosophers, proceed by analyzing phenomena into discrete units and then recombining them by general principles. He contrasted the method of analysis and recomposition with intuition which grasps events as they appear and then dialectically relates them in more or less adequate descriptions (for example, by the relation of mutual complementarity and mutual antagonism). Intuitive analysis never succeeds in reproducing concrete existence: it must use language to construct spatialized images that can only allude to what is actually experienced. It describes variations on themes rather than identities. Political relations are based on the analysis that human beings carry out on themselves when they separate themselves from others and distinguish between "I" and "you," "mine" and "yours." The division is recomposed by making oneself the other to oneself or by making the other submit to oneself as an instrument. The closest approximation to an intuitively-based solidarity is a fully committed act of generosity, which is the polar opposite of the political relation. In generosity a particular self assimilates the particular strivings of the other and translates them immediately into a deed. Between the purely political relation and the generous deed is a series of solidarities which are based on different types and degrees of appreciation of particularity, relativity, and dependence.

143

THE EXPLOSION OF MEANING (2)

Political relations are justified by the deepest and most basic social truth that knowledge is not virtue. The universal practical acknowledgment of interdependence does not always (to put it mildly) result in active acceptance of it resulting in voluntary mutual aid and mutual appreciation. All have some of Dostoevsky's "underground man" in them: all strive in some instances and some strive in most instances to assert their individual reflective temporality over and against other human beings, either by exploiting them or by defending themselves against exploitation or even against being absorbed by gifts. Political orders are ways of containing the rebellion against solidarity, usually in the Hobbesian fashion of satiating some exploiters at the expense of others. The "elite theorists," such as Mosca, Pareto, and Michels gave an accurate description of pure politics, in which all other forms of human solidarity are *used as means* to enforce control in space: meanings are made myths, functions are made interests, and appreciations are made stimuli. The elite theorists were correct in paying so much attention to the "political formula" or "legitimating myth" because meaningful solidarity is the closest and, therefore, the most easily manipulated form of union to the formal and mechanical solidarities of pure politics.

Meaningful solidarity is the community constituted by what has been called throughout the preceding discussion a commitment to "cultural time perspectives." Joint acceptance of a system of transpersonal meaning results in each one acknowledging the other as a participant in a common effort or experience, not merely as an abstract subject of rights and duties or object of power. Each is related to the other through a project in time rather than through a static rule or an immediate threat. Meaningful solidarity is felt by the individual as "consciousness of kind." This feeling can be exploited in political processes as a means to mobilize people to protect their advantages over other groups or to wrest advantages away from other groups, but it can also be the awareness of more concrete processes such as functional interdependence and mutual appreciation. Meaningful

144

solidarity generates a "we" that is lacking in pure politics. Sometimes the "we" results from the negative project of defense or resistance, in which case it tends to break down rapidly into political processes, while at other times the "we" is common awareness of a distinctive history and participation in a defined destiny.

The collapse of cultural time perspectives in the present era has meant their increased exploitation in political processes aimed merely at control and advantage. What is at stake in Northern Ireland, Cyprus, Lebanon, and Nigeria? Is it the survival of religious communities or retention of systematic advantages? Are the religious systems of transpersonal meaning in these cases merely mobilization and consolidation myths or are they the reasons for the conflicts? The answers to these questions are probably ambiguous, but the fact that they can be raised seriously indicates the depth of the crisis of meaning. Cultural time perspectives are in question not only because of their relativity to one another, but because they are so readily exploited by states and movements. "Consciousness of kind" is a commodity on the political market that is advertised and "sold," often at the point of a gun.

Meaningful solidarity occurs in the spatialized time of culture, not the abstract clock time of law and politics. When meaningful solidarity is intense it limits and qualifies political relations by providing people with an implicit confidence that others will not act in unexpected ways and that others will experience internal limits on what they will do to assert themselves. It generates feelings of at-homeness, familiarity, and comfort that put people at ease, dampen down their anxiety, and relax their guard. Although there is little meaningful solidarity in modern states, some still exists in sheltered neighborhoods whose residents are socio-economically homogeneous and share common aspirations. The emphasis by systems theorists and functionalists on normative consensus indicates its absence, as do the frenetic appeals to draw meaning from imminent military or ecological disaster, or from the grand historical project of redistributing material resources. Neither ideology nor utopia is today what it once was. Both have been reduced to reflections on persistence in physical space.

Meaningful solidarity often conceals another form of unity that makes it possible. Durkheim identified organic solidarity as that kind of union based on interdependence of objective and primarily economic functions. The division of labor had, according to him, created a situation in which human beings were incapable of taking individual responsibility for the totality of activities that sustained their common life. All depended on each for the ability to mount and maintain projects. Each was an extension of the other, completing the other's life by providing something necessary or desirable to it. For Durkheim and his predecessors like Proudhon and Kropotkin, organic solidarity was not only an objective fact but the principle of a social ethic. They realized that both capitalism and socialism were not economic systems but varieties of the political relation, subordinating production and use to ownership, control, and advantage. They held that the essence of the economic relation was cooperation and mutual aid. The problem that beset those who identified organic solidarity was that of knowledge and virtue. It was obvious that human beings were not self sufficient and self reliant, and that no single group could constitute the public situation by itself, but acknowledgment of these facts did not necessarily result in active acceptance of them. Human beings could and did seek to gain advantage over one another, groups could strive for domination and monopoly over meaning, and institutions could be devised to ratify systematic exploitation. As Elijah Jordan, who based his social and political philosophy on organic solidarity, said: "Men can see, but they cannot do."

Active acceptance of organic solidarity depends upon an interpretation of the category of "need." Each must act with the object of maintaining the entire system of interdependence by refraining from taking advantage of the other

146

through such means as force, threat, fraud, bribery, flattery, or ridicule. One must lend trust to the other and avoid making the other resentful. The basis of social morality here is recognition of mutual need. One needs the other to complete one's projects. Yet active acceptance of organic solidarity is fragile. In exploitative orders based primarily on the political relation, functional interdependence is transformed into competition among interests. Appeals to cooperation and mutuality are used as propaganda for bolstering up established institutional patterns. Each one is identified with a series of groups that seek to demonstrate their indispensability by threats, strikes, and the more silent means of budgetary allocations. Active acceptance of organic solidarity in pluralistic competitive systems or in single-party directive systems often results in self destruction. Simple responsibility, not to mention generosity, becomes objectively foolhardy and a sign of mental disorder.

Even if the economic order were not subordinated to the *political* relations of capitalism (profit) and socialism (control), organic solidarity would still not be a sufficient basis for human unity. There would always be questions about what functions shoud be included in the public situation, how much resources should be allocated to them, who should have access to what facilities and products. Moreover, even the most generous conceptions of organic solidarity exclude those who are incapable or unwilling to perform a useful social function. The "loose ends" of organic solidarity are normally knit together by meaningful solidarity, which provides an object for which each function exists, and the political relation, which determines a final order in space. The measure in which people actively accept organic solidarity indicates their willingness and ability to dispense with the more abstract and limiting types of union. Yet the only "principle" of organic solidarity is continuation of a stable equilibrium or harmony of functions: a prescription for stagnation, death, and eternal recurrence. Organic solidarity can be qualified on one boundary by meaning or advantage and on the other boundary by appreciation.

THE EXPLOSION OF MEANING (2)

Active acceptance of organic solidarity involves conceiving of oneself as a more particular, dependent, and relative being than either the formal solidarity of politics or the meaningful solidarity of cultural time perspectives allow. An even greater awareness of one's fundamental sociality is implied by the process of appreciation in which we express one another's lives to each other. Social relations reach their perfection when we base active acceptance of organic solidarity upon appreciation rather than upon common meaning, equal freedoms, or fear and advantage. Organic solidarity signifies that we need others in order to maintain an individual life, regardless of its content, while appreciation signifies that we need others to provide us with the very contents that we express and then reflect into the past-present-future. Those who have understood the dangers of unchecked political relations have attempted to restore meaningful solidarity. This approach has led to the dead end of total war, genocide, concentration camps, imperialism, nuclear stalemate, drives to autarky and hegemony, and crisis politics. Appreciation provides an alternative life principle to meaning, but it is so distant from the political relation that it seems impossible to make it serve even as a leaven in the public situation.

Perhaps Heidegger was correct that we live in an interregnum between the death of our old gods and the birth of new ones. Perhaps our system of organizational conflict is such that all embryonic gods (meanings) will be automatically aborted by their manipulation as myths and idols. Today any politics that does not lead towards deprivation and death must be based on sacrifice of interests and privileges: it must be the reversal of politics as we have known it in the modern age and probably since the beginnings of civilization. Sacrifice is not generosity, although it is based upon appreciation of the other's disadvantages and awareness of the allowances that must be made if these disadvantages are to be overcome. Sacrifice is active acceptance of the commitment to expand the ability of the other to express one's own life. It acknowledges that those who have been treated stereotypi-

148

cally must be treated categorically (given compensations) if they are to become aware of their own concrete durational being. Sacrifice, then, is not only the transfer of resources, but the transfusion of experience. Yet it seems ridiculous even to speak about it under the shadow of contemporary macropolitics.

We live in an age when knowledge of the conditions of our existence does not lead to virtue, when even the most enlightened *self* interest directs us towards annihilation. Each of us is a concrete durational being, more or less jealous of our specious independence, more or less consumed by the hunger for immortality, more or less resentful about the injuries that have been inflicted upon us. We hate the arbitrary nature of politics, but flee to politics to protect ourselves from those to whom we have done injury. The most enlightened among us concoct abstract schemes of justice, new meanings for humanity, and vitriolic critiques of depersonalization. We retain the belief that there is still hope in "leading from strength," in setting things right *ourselves.* I speak as someone who knows our mentality by having lived it and continuing to live it. A privileged white male is defined by the desire always to lead from strength. He does not even want to admit that he might like to make a sacrifice unless, of course, that sacrifice has cosmic or, at least, historical significance. Is the idea of an oppressor's liberation a null set? If so, we have all doomed ourselves to destroy the selves that we cherish so much.

Notes

Chapter I

1. Rene Descartes, "Discourse," in *Descartes: Selections,* ed. Ralph Eaton (New York: Charles Scribner's Sons, 1927), p. 9.

2. Ibid.

3. Feodor Dostoevsky, *The Brothers Karamazov* (New York: New American Library, 1957), p. 235.

4. Thomas Hobbes, *Leviathan: Parts I and II* (Indianapolis: Bobbs-Merrill, 1958), pp. 106-7.

5. Elijah Jordan, *The Good Life* (Chicago: University of Chicago Press, 1952), p. 90.

6. Karl Marx and Friedrich Engels, *The Communist Manifesto* (New York: Appleton-Century-Crofts, 1955), p. 37.

7. Ibid., p. 38.

8. Max Scheler, *Ressentiment* (New York: Schocken Books, 1961), p. 72.

9. Karl Mannheim, *Ideology and Utopia* (New York: Harvest Books, n.d.), p. 41.

10. Ibid., p. 45.

11. Ibid., p. 8.

12. Ibid., p. 94.

13. Ibid., p. 87.

14. George Herbert Mead, *The Philosophy of the Present* (LaSalle: Open Court Publishing Company, 1959), p. 1.

15. Robert Duncan, "Man's Fulfillment in Order and Strife," *Caterpillar* 8/9 (1969): 241.

150

NOTES

16. Josiah Royce, *The World and the Individual* (New York: Dover, 1959), p. 172.

17. Ibid., p. 182.

18. Ibid., pp. 182–83.

19. Alejandro Korn, "La Libertad Creadora," in Korn, *La Libertad Creadora* (Buenos Aires: Editorial Claridad, 1963), p. 98.

20. Alejandro Korn, "Introducción al estudio de Kant," in Korn, *Filósofos y Sistemas* (Buenos Aires: Colección Claridad, n.d.), p. 57.

21. Teodoro Olarte Sáenz del Castillo, "Alejandro Korn ante el Problema de la Metafísica," in *Estudios sobre Alejandro Korn* (La Plata: Universidad Nacional de la Plata, 1973), p. 96.

22. Charles Sanders Peirce, "How to Make our Ideas Clear," in Peirce, *Essays in the Philosophy of Science* (Indianapolis: Bobbs-Merrill, 1957), 42–43n.

23. Ibid., 43–44n.

24. E.H. Carr, *The Twenty Years' Crisis: 1919–1939* (London: Macmillan, 1961), p. 160.

25. Descartes, "Discourse," p. 21.

26. Alberto Zum Felde, *Proceso Intelectual del Uruguay* (Montevideo: Editorial Claridad, 1941), p. 379.

27. Friedrich Georg Juenger, *The Failure of Technology* (Chicago: Henry Regnery, 1956), p. 48.

28. Ibid., p. 49.

29. Agustín Basave Fernández del Valle, *Filosofía del Hombre* (México: Espasa-Calpe, 1963), p. 135.

30. Ibid., p. 134.

Chapter II

1. Henri Bergson, *Time and Free Will* (New York: Harper and Row, 1960), p. 128.

2. G.W.F. Leibniz, "A Universal Character," in *Leibniz: Selections,* ed. Philip Weiner (New York: Charles Scribner's Sons, 1951), p. 20.

3. Ibid., p. 19.

4. Immanuel Kant, *Prolegomena to a Metaphysics of Morals* (Indianapolis: Bobbs-Merrill, 1956), p. 69.

5. Ibid., p. 72.

NOTES

6. Henri Bergson, "The Perception of Change," in Bergson, *The Creative Mind* (New York: Philosophical Library, 1946), p. 138.

7. Ibid., p. 137.

8. Bergson, *Time and Free Will,* p. 134.

9. Henri Bergson, *Creative Evolution* (New York: Random House, 1944), p. 274.

10. Henri Bergson, *The Two Sources of Morality and Religion* (New York: Doubleday and Co., n.d.), p. 119.

11. Ibid., p. 119.

12. Bergson, *Time and Free Will,* p. 136.

13. Ibid., p. 138.

14. Ibid., p. 231.

15. Benedetto Croce, *Aesthetic* (New York: Noonday Press, 1960), p. 112.

16. Bergson, *Creative Evolution,* p. 249.

17. Max Stirner, *The Ego and His Own* (New York: Boni and Liveright, n.d.), p. 147.

18. Ibid., p. 148.

19. Ibid., p. 231.

20. Miguel de Unamuno, *The Tragic Sense of Life* (New York: Dover, 1954), p. 45.

21. Ibid., p. 256.

22. Ibid., p. 240.

Chapter III

1. Nikos Kazantzakis, *Zorba the Greek* (New York: Simon and Schuster, 1959), p. 175.

2. Nikos Kazantzakis, *The Last Temptation of Christ* (New York: Bantam Books, 1965), p. 1.

3. Nikos Kazantzakis, *Report to Greco* (New York: Bantam Books, 1971), p. 376.

4. Ibid., p. 414.

5. Nikos Kazantzakis, *The Saviors of God* (New York: Simon and Schuster, 1960), p. 68.

6. Kazantzakis, *Report to Greco,* p. 358.

NOTES

7. Kazantzakis, *Zorba the Greek,* pp. 225-26.
8. Kazantzakis, *Report to Greco,* p. 453.
9. Ibid., p. 457.
10. Ibid., p. 401.
11. Ibid.
12. Ibid., p. 470.

Chapter IV

1. Miguel de Unamuno, *The Tragic Sense of Life* (New York: Dover, 1954), p. 445.

Indexes

Index of Names

154

INDEX

Index of Terms

155

INDEX